THE ENCHANTMENTS OF BRITAIN

K. E. Maltwood, F. R. S. A.

James Clarke & Co
Cambridge

This edition 1982

ISBN 0 227 67832 X

Published by:
**James Clarke & Co. Ltd
7 All Saints' Passage
Cambridge, CB2 3LS
England**

Printed in Great Britain by
Redwood Burn Ltd., Trowbridge, Wiltshire and
bound by Pegasus Bookbinding, Melksham, Wiltshire.

CONTENTS

LIST OF ILLUSTRATIONS

PART I

The zodiacal giants of Somerset and the
respective celestial constellations
The circle shows the ecliptic of the equinox at 2700 B.C.

1. A PREHISTORIC ZODIAC IN ENGLAND

The zodiacal constellations had been long established when the sun entered the 'sign' Aries at the vernal equinox, but no explanation has been vouchsafed that could account for the notoriety of these 'signs' down the ages. So the question was: when were they designed, and where, and how, and by whom? Ptolemy (A.D. 150) transmits them from Hipparchus (130 B.C.) 'as of unquestioned authority, unknown origin, and unsearchable antiquity.'

Historical astronomers realized that the zodiacal constellation 'creatures' did not originate on the ceiling of a temple, the dome of a mosque, or the pavement of a church, where they are still found in many places. The universality of the design proves that the civilization that engendered these signs must have had ramifications not only through Europe, Egypt and the Near East, but through India, Persia and the East Indies, wherever sun worship penetrated. They also know that star gazers could only observe these particular constellations, through which the sun rides, in a region answering to Asia Minor, and not so far south as Egypt.

The discovery of a great zodiac laid out among the little hills in the neighbourhood of Glastonbury, in Somerset, England, seems to answer the above queries, for here is apparently the first 'Mighty Labour of the Isle of Britain' of which the Welsh bards sang.[1] It has lain prone on the ground for thousands of years, covered with King Arthur's fabled 'mantle of invisibility', though seeing everyone.

The explanation as to who made it is that the Cymry of Wales came, according to their traditions, 'from the East in the Age of Ages', (Barddas) bringing the knowledge of the stars from Asia Minor, and laid out this zodiac, which they called in the Welsh tongue *Caer Sidi*. Dr. L. A. Waddell confirms their tradition in his *Makers of Civilization*. He says (page 6): 'Detailed proofs are given in my former works for the Sumerian origin of the Cymry with approximate dates for the Sumerian mining and colonizing occupation of parts of the British Isles by several immigrations from the Sargonic period of about 2700 B.C. onwards.'

The sophistication of the design of this 'Round Table of the Stars' shows that it was laid out by experts, for no artistic, religious or scientific conception combined with agriculture could transcend its expression. It is artistic in its beautiful composition and virile drawing, religious in that it reflects God's universe and laws, scientific in its stellar observations and geometrical layout. With the 'Children of the Sun' their religion and science were at one.

During thousands of years the zodiac was so much revered that every figure there portrayed was a sacred emblem; for instance, the four evangelistic symbols of the Bull, Lion, Man and Bird are found here in Somerset in their proper places at the four cardinal points — Taurus, Leo, Sagittarius and Aquarius[2] — whereas on modern maps there is no bird amongst the zodiacal constellations. It follows that these Christian symbols were founded on this original design, and correspond to the standard of Sargon II, King of Assyria.[3]

Temples as we understand them were not great enough to contain the constellations; so mother Nature was chosen to sustain them, and the thirty-mile circumference of this sacred area was looked upon in its beginning as the 'Cauldron of unfailing supply': it had three properties — inexhaustibility, inspiration, and regeneration. We are told by the Welsh bards, the descendants of the Cymry, that it was stolen from the 'Divine Land' for it was Annwn itself. Taliesin, who knew most about it, sings in *The Spoils of Annwn*[4] of the recovery by Arthur of the magic Cauldron of inspiration and that it was found at Caer Sidi, the zodiac.

This Cauldron was associated with a Druid cult before it became the Christian Grail; both in Norman romance and Welsh literature it possessed the same characteristics.

> I have been teacher to all the universe;
> I shall be until the day of doom on the face of the earth;
> I have been in a toilsome chair above the Zodiac,
> Which revolves between three elements,

Is it not a wonder that the world discerns me not?

Taliesin was the 'official' bard of the mysteries of this Caer Sidi, and boasts he was present with Arthur when he stole the Cauldron; he was also the son of the goddess of the Cauldron. When Merlin entered the glass house the treasure of Britain vanished with him, the plentiful feeding vessels with the rest;[5] thus what has now been recovered was thought to have been lost though it was said to have been capable of feeding all the world.[6]

In *The Arthurian Legend* by John Rhys (page 345) we read: 'But we are here more particularly interested in Glastonbury, the identification of which with Avallach's Isle, and all that term was supposed to connote would naturally lead to the further conclusion that it was also the "Land of Summer", which in the form *Somerset* has become fixed as the name of the county to which Glastonbury belongs.'

So it is not surprising that Somerset yielded up the secrets of the Summer[7] country and that the discovery of the 'Star Giants' was the result of making maps to illustrate the twelfth-century romance called *The High History of the Holy Grail*.

Thus in tracing the quest of the Knights of the Round Table between the famous Avalon Isle, King Arthur's Castle of Camelot, and Wales, it was found that Sir Lancelot and the other knights quested roughly in a circle over the same ground, encountering a Lion, Giants, and a fiery Dragon.

Years of puzzling over the mystery as to what they were really questing, obviously not a Christian Grail, revealed that the Cary River in its windings drew the outline of a Lion, the two Dundon hills formed a Giant, and so on. Thus here were Knights hunting 'Nature Gods', but they themselves were the Christian reincarnations of the gods they quested, or perhaps astrologers might say they were born under those particular stars, Sir Lancelot showing all the characteristics of the Lion, King Arthur of the sun god Hercules, Sir Gawain of the Ram, etc.

This then explained 'the wonders of Great Britain', and 'the great adventurers of the Kingdom of Logres'[8] for here we have a dual myth of earth and sky — the star

constellations laid out on earth, and the Knights imperson-
ating the stars above them. A magnificent conception!

The Description of this Zodiac
So it is in Somerset, England, that we have discovered
what King Arthur's *System of the Round Table* really was.
A Guide to Glastonbury's Temple of the Stars and its *Air
View Supplement* fully illustrates and describes it.[9]

This zodiac, or agricultural calendar, is surrounded on
three sides by hills, about one thousand feet high, which
are crowned by prehistoric forts. On the west flows the
Severn sea with Wales on the opposite shore. Within this
natural enclosure, the low-lying hills are shaped to form
the star constellation giants.

Outlining the design to a great extent are two small
rivers that have not changed their course, being penned in
by the little hills of this mysterious Kingdom of Logres, as
The High History of the Holy Grail calls it.

From the realistic drawing of the 'Creatures', which are
superb in outline, from the demonstrated knowledge of
irrigation, and earthwork construction of a high order,
from the apparent date of the equinox, about 2700 B.C.,
and from tradition, this planisphere strongly suggests the
culture of the Euphrates, and has no connection with the
monolithic stone monuments of Avebury and Stonehenge.

In order that the design should fit the dome of the sky
and the twelve zodiacal divisions of the calendar, with
their corresponding stars, the figures are so arranged as to
contract towards the centre of the circle of signs; an
amazing achievement considering that most of them
measure three miles long, but the whole composition is
astonishingly skilful.

As the Lion and Scorpion[9] were then double the size
they are now represented on star maps, they here occupy
the place of the Crab and Scales respectively as well as
their own.

The figures lying towards the north of the circle
represent the winter months — the Scorpion, Archer, Goat,
Water-carrier and Fishes attached to the Whale.

Opposite are — the Ram, Bull, Twins, Lion and Virgin.
Thus they correspond in regard to their order, as they do in

their traditional characteristics, with those seen on astronomical globes in use at the present day; but the modern copies of these constellations have lost the rhythm and meaning of the original conception.

For instance, the drama of these winter months is that the Scorpion of death has stung the Archer's horse, ,causing it to fall forward as this old sun-god shoots his last ray into the 'Bull's Eye'. In consequence he dismounts from his horse's neck, giving the impression of a centaur as on modern star pictures.

The feet of both horse and rider are already hidden by the earth sign Capricornus, for the Archer represents the end of the year; thus the sun-god has 'one foot in the grave', for the great earthwork forming the Goat's bronze age horn is called locally 'the Golden Coffin' and the stars that correspond are Job's Coffin. In accordance with Druid belief and mediaeval art, the Whale lies in wait for his soul, mouth open towards the pole of the ecliptic, and this Whale is the only effigy constellation thus to face east. It is entirely outlined by waterways.

The Water-carrier, being an air sign, is here represented by a Phoenix, holding the vessel of water in its beak. It is fanning its burning nest with its outstretched wings. Glastonbury's famous Isle of Avalon, towering 600 feet out of the marsh, forms this bird, and the Urn contains the life-giving 'blood spring' known far and wide as Chalice Well; its waters are radio-active and stain the stones over which it flows blood red.

'The First Church of Britain', that is to say the wattle Chapel of St. Joseph of Arimathea, and afterwards Glastonbury Abbey, were built upon the tail of this Phoenix. Consequently it was hallowed ground long before the pagan king gave it to the Christians; for the Isle of Avalon was known through Europe as the 'Island of the Blest, Avalon, the place of departed spirits'.[10] There is much legendary history connected with the subject, but all we can touch on now is its foundation in the 'Round Table of the Stars'.

To continue its description: after the Fish, the young Ram and the Bull, the drama of the summer months is the apotheosis of the regenerated sun and nature represented by the solar babe sitting in his moon boat, for the first Twins were the sun and moon. Around him cluster adoring animals — the Bull, Lion, Little Dog, and Griffon, which is part of the rudder of the Ship; whilst the Virgin with outstretched wheatsheaf offers to him the fruits of the earth on bended knee.

The unusual features of the whole composition are: first, that the only human beings represented are the Father, Mother and Child, and that the old bearded sun-god Hercules, who rides the horse of Sagittarius, points with the first finger of his right hand to the exact centre of the circle of the signs, but this centre is neither the pole of the ecliptic, nor that of the pole star Thuban (Alpha Draconis). This finger is repeated on a much larger scale in order to lie along the line of the equinox, pointing directly into the eye of the Bull and in alignment with the royal stars, Aldebaran and Antares in Scorpio.

Another very marked feature of the design is that the heads of eleven figures turn towards the sunset over the sea which lies due west, for the equinoctial line between Aldebaran and Antares runs west and east.

When designing this chart of the stars, as much emphasis was laid on the path of the sun as upon the position of the equinox, for the 'Solar Babe' with upraised arm holds on to the central line of the ecliptic by the two stars of Gemini that lie upon it.[11] The Virgin's Wheatsheaf and the Ram's (traditionally) reverted head are made to measure the width of the sun's path, and the Bull and Lion point it out with their right feet and the Lion's tongue, which is an interesting feature, being made of red earth.

The astonishing knowledge and skill displayed in laying out these star figures on the earth places this solar calendar in a unique position in regard to archaeological survivals, hence the traditional sanctity of the neighbourhood around Glastonbury, 'The Temple of the British Secret Tradition'[12] for it constituted a laboratory of thought and mystery, recognized by the races of the continent of Europe as unspeakably hallowed and inscrutable.

The astronomer M. Proctor remarks: 'Learned

antiquarians have searched every page of heathen mythology, and ransacked legend, poetry and fable, in a vain endeavour to discover who were the inventors of the constellations, but without avail.' So the subject of the origin of these signs is full of interest to the chronologist who inquires into what era of the world exact astronomy began and when the sun was assigned his twelve zodiacal constellations.

The discovery of this unique zodiac should solve the problems of when, where and how the constellations were designed, and English history points the direction from whence the inventors came. 'Hu the Mighty' had brought the Cymry from the Summer country to the Isle of Britain in the 'Age of Ages'; after which the first king of Britain was of the royal house of Troy.[13] When he was sent to 'Albion' this Brutus was told that there were giants in the land, supposedly Hercules, Orion and the rest of these giants born of heaven and earth.

Troy in Asia Minor fulfils all the conditions laid down by Maunder, such as, the region from which the stars of these particular constellations were observed, the animals chosen to represent them and the knowledge of ship building.

Brute — past the realms of Gaul, beyond the sunset
Lieth an Island, girt about by ocean,
Guarded by ocean — erst the haunt of giants,
Desert of late, and meet for this thy people.
Seek it! For there is thine abode for ever;
There by thy sons again shall Troy be builded;
There of thy blood shall Kings be born, hereafter
Sovran in every land the wide world over.[14]

2. MAN'S OLDEST SCIENTIFIC HEIRLOOM

Thereafter, the dark warning of our King,
That most of us would follow wandering fires,
Came like a driving gloom across my mind.

Tennyson's Holy Grail

In my grandfather's day most sizable houses had their star globe, and children delighted in chasing the constellation creatures as they spun round on its zodiacal belt, shouting the well-known adage — the Ram, the Bull, the Heavenly Twins, next to the Crab, the Lion shines, the Virgin and the Scales, the Scorpion, Archer and Sea Goat, the man that bears the Water Pot and Fish with glittering scales. But nowadays an astronomical sphere is a curiosity, whilst the zodiacal jingle is forgotten.[1] Can we wonder that this 'oldest scientific heirloom of the human race' finds the present generation nonplussed when they are told its original conception — the prehistoric chart of the heavens has been found in England.

Perhaps the easiest way to learn what this chart of the sky means is to describe a circle, divide it into twelve equal parts from its centre and draw in each division one of the above named creatures in correct order, making sure the proper stars fall within each figure. This exercise gives one considerable respect for the genius, of 5,000 years ago, who designed the circular composition to fit the 'fixed' stars which is still being used today.

Having thus visualized this celestial circle, let us picture ourselves inside it and being turned round to gaze at its constellations during the whole of the twenty-four hour day — for if the sun were eclipsed during daylight hours we could see this procession of the stars continuously repeating through the year — and probably that is how the Chaldeans found it out, for they made records of eclipses of the sun for hundreds of years before our era and had a picture of the zodiacal figures in their mind's eye.

As we on earth are also moving round the sun once in a

year, the sun is seen (during partial eclipses) against a different background every month, e.g., the Ram, or the Bull, etc; that was the reason for the expression 'the sun in Scorpio' or the other eleven constellations: but now what are called the 'signs' no longer have the same relation to the stars on account of the precession of the equinoxes, and when I say the sun was in the Bull when these figures were laid out upon the earth, I imply that it was there every spring equinox for 2,000 years, after which at the spring equinox it had moved into the Ram, and is now in fact in the stars of the Fish close to the Water Carrier; though the almanac will tell us the sun enters 'the sign' of the Ram on 21 March!

Having stepped inside our drawing of the star creatures we can picture how the ancients first laid it out upon the earth, using the little hills and rivers to suggest the effigy animals and human beings, completing their features by modelling earthworks on them to represent their ears, horns, jaws, paws or whatever was lacking. This model was laid out in the county of Somerset, which name, with its tidal River Parrett, is derived from the Sumerian language; so the folk who planned it were presumably clay modellers from the valley of the Euphrates and Asia Minor, at that time in what is known archaeologically as the Bronze Age.

Nimrod was the first really great ruler of ancient Babylon which city was then the most important centre in the known world; at the height of its glory, one of its temples was called 'The Temple of the Foundation of Heaven and Earth', for Marduk, who was the same person as Nimrod, 'made the first design of the stars, he regulated the course of the whole universe on the move-ment of the sun. He instituted the year and divided it into twelve months in order that all the gods should have their image visible in the sky', according to the clay tablets.[1]

Consequently, might it be possible that Nimrod was the mighty one upon the earth who laid out the zodiac in Somerset — which is the Round Table of King Arthur and his Knights — for Wolfram von Eschenbach tells us that the father of Parzival, the hero of the Grail Quest, was killed fighting Babylon's princes for the king of Bagdad; of these princes he says, 'From Ninus they came, who was ruler ere ever Bagdad might be, Nineveh did he found', and Masonic tradition says that Nimrod built Nineveh. Parzival was also the son of that 'widow lady' who was a Welsh Queen. (See Wolfram's Herzeleid.)

In *The Makers of Civilization* Dr. Waddell tells us so much about the Sumerian kings, and their connection with The British Edda which he translated from ninth-century manuscripts, that we need only say here that Nimrod was the second Sumerian king canonized in Chaldea. 'He was the historical original of the legendary culture hero greatly extending agriculture and inventing the plough.' Sargon's ships reached the tin mines 'beyond the Western Sea' or Mediterranean, presumably in Cornwall.

Berosus inscribed Marduk's name at the beginning of his book, when he set about relating to the Greeks the origin of the world according to the Chaldeans, and the dawn of Babylonian civilization; Berosus was a priest of Babylon about 200 B.C. who made use of the archives in the temple of Bel at Babylon. Mr. Harding reminds us in the *Journal of Calendar Reform* with regard to Babylonian astrologers that 'About 4,000 years ago, when the Bull was the first constellation of the Zodiac, the Chaldeans made very accurate measurements of time. Our information about their calendar and their astronomical observations has been obtained from an ancient work called *The Observations of Bell* supposed to date from about 1,700 B.C. consisting of seven hundred books written on small earthern tablets.'

So as regards their ecliptic, or path of the sun drawn through the constellation figures of the 'fixed' stars along which the sun and moon invariably ride, it is on this path that the Knights of King Arthur rode in quest of the Holy Grail: herein lies the mystery of that vast field of legend pertaining to the Isle of Avalon which by the aid of my specialized training I have endeavoured to elucidate, during twenty-five years' search on the actual ground and on maps and air views of this enchanted land of Arthurian Romance.

I lay claim to the discovery, delineation and localization of these effigy constellation giants: my subsequent speculations and suggestions are feelers put forth in the hope of attracting more light upon an obscure but universal subject, for now that the riddle as to the object of the Quest has been solved and localized in the neighbour-hood of Glastonbury, we can look to others to settle the debatable questions.

Now let us consider the acknowledged connection between Freemasonry and the Quest of the Grail. To begin with, every Temple or Masonic Lodge should have its celestial and terrestrial spheres as essential equipment, so there is no excuse for Freemasons who have attained to the Holy Royal Arch not grasping the tremendous import to them of the discovery of 'the ancient landmarks' of this star temple laid out in the face of sun and eye of light; their secrets, ritual, symbols and jewels will be found to apply once the question has been properly understood. For instance, as regards its founder, the *Speculative Mason* says under Notes and Queries, 'The old Operative Masons looked upon Nimrod[2] as the first great builder and Mason; he organized the Craft, taught them measures and gave them Charges. The Cook MS. which was copied down about 1,430 tells how Nimrod began the Tower of Babylon, with 40,000 workmen who also builded the City of Nineveh, and in this manner the Craft of Masonry was first perfected and charged for a science and a craft.' He was the Son of Cush who some say was the progenitor of the Sumer-Akkad people. It is possible the Knights of King Arthur were also questing lost Masonic secrets!

Without further comment let me quote from the *Holy Grail* (pp. 485-86) written by a great student of secret traditions of like nature, Arthur E. Waite:

While Masonry itself does not less represent an active power at work, within its own measures, because it has only substitutes to offer in respect of great things unrealized, and pictures in place of reality; ... it follows from all the Traditional Histories, all the Symbolism ... and in fine from all the Rituals of Masonry ... that they looked for the return of that which, for the time, had been taken away; ... that when they mourn over the Holy Sepulchre, they were never more certain that what has been removed is alive ... all Degrees end in a substituted restoration. The word is always restored: that which was lost according to the record of the Master Guild is recovered in the Royal Arch.[3] In other words, it is the intimation of Secret Schools that somewhere in time and the world there is that which can confer upon the Candidate a real as well as a symbolic experience. And this is the identical message of the Grail literature.

That is his considered opinion after a long life's inquiry, and again he says, it is:

as if something were guiding and consoling all the Keepers of the Keys, but dissuading them at the same time from opening certain doors till that which has been lost is at length restored to the Sanctuaries. It is in this sense only that we shall ever get to understand the Inner Mystery of the Holy Grail, the Mystery of the Craft Degrees and of the great, disordered cohort of things from near and far — reflections, rumours, replicas and suppositious descents from older Mysteries — which make up the cloud of witnesses in the High Degrees. . . . I conclude, that it is an index-finger pointing to other Rites, to greater and exalted Ceremonies, which — somewhat shadowy, somewhat dubious, yet distinguishable as to their purpose — remain among the records of the past, not without suggestions that, even at this day, the Mysteries have not died utterly.

For one book he is lamenting,
Which he loves more than gold and precious stones
The fair Grail of this country.
A book of the famed Knights
A book of Mystery of all the Round Table.

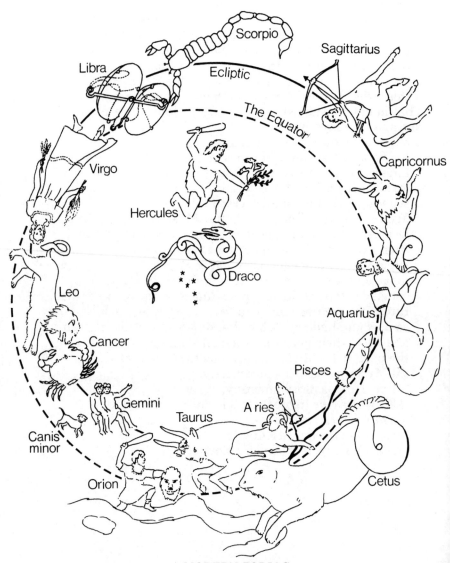

Scorpio

Sagittarius

Libra

Ecliptic

The Equator

Virgo

Capricornus

Hercules

Draco

Aquarius

Leo

Pisces

Cancer

Gemini

A ries

Taurus

Canis
minor

Cetus

Orion

A MODERN ZODIAC
The ship Argo is omitted from the lower left-hand corner
where it should be sailing into the circle.

3. THE CALENDAR OF 4,700 YEARS AGO

No signs they knew to mark the wintry year:
The flower strewn Spring, and the fruit-laden Summer,
Uncalendared, unregistered, returned —
Till I the difficult art of the stars revealed,
Their rising and their setting. Numbers, too,
I taught them (a most choice device) and how
By marshalled signs to fix their shifting thought,
That Memory, mother of Muses, might achieve
Her wondrous work.

Aeschylus. *Prometheus Bound*

A thousand ages in Thy sight are but as yesterday when it is past, but for the agriculturist his very existence depends on Time's ordered sequence because of seed time and harvest, consequently it is interesting to consider how the ancients first planned the arrangements of the zodiacal constellations with the calendar, and thus drew order out of chaos.

The Sumer-Chaldeans, by laboriously studying the infallible laws that govern the stellar universe, had learned so to trust them not to change that they conceived of a pattern to fit the stars along the circular path of the sun, consisting of a series of figures representing living creatures.

In the case of the Temple of the Stars in Somerset, colossal labour was entailed in shaping the hills and rivers to this pattern, with an astonishing knowledge of astronomy, geometry and geodesy. Irrigation also played a large part in its conception, as it was necessary to increase the fertility of the sacred area, because these nature sculptures represented the sky gods of supreme power and the crops to be grown on their bodies had to be phenomenal, in so much that *The High History of the Holy Grail* tells us: 'they had such great abundance there within of everything they could desire that naught in the world was there whereof they lacked'; that was the characteristic of the Grail from the beginning, for in the Bardic *Book of Taliesin* Arthur gained possession of a magic cauldron —

a pagan Keltic type of the Holy Grail — which furnished inexhaustible food, though 'it will not boil the food of a coward'. The Cauldron found at Caer Sidi (the Zodiac), an island of immortal youth amid 'the streams of the ocean' where 'there is a food-giving fountain'. It would appear that the Cauldron was itself the Zodiac.

This vast circle of effigies must be the original design for the signs lying along the Ecliptic that are in use today almost unchanged, and is therefore of inestimable value archaeologically and historically, for no other configuration of the earth's surface could conform to the same pattern in such a way. The stars themselves fall roughly into the corresponding effigies, but do not make any shape in the sky, as can be seen, hence the supposition that this layout was the original design for the present zodiac.

Maspero, in speaking of Chaldean formulas and figures for land-surveying, says: 'Actual knowledge was woven in an extraordinary manner with mystic considerations, in which the virtues of numbers, their connections with the gods, and the application of geometrical diagrams to the prediction of the future, played an important part. . . . It was a question in ancient times whether the Chaldeans or the Egyptians had been the first to carry their investigations into the infinite depths of celestial space; when it came to be a Question as to which of the two peoples had made the greater progress in this branch of knowledge, all hesitation vanished and the pre-eminence was accorded by the ancients to the priests of Babylon rather than to those of Heliopolis and Memphis.'

We know from the Babylonian clay tablets preserved in the British Museum, that this astronomical priestly knowledge existed before the time of Khammurabi, famous for his Code of Laws derived from very early Sumerian code still extant; his influence in 1950 B.C. extended from the Indus Valley through Mesopatamia, Egypt and Crete. But fortunately we do not have to rely only on history for the date of the zodiacal lay-out, as the design itself gives it to us.

Robert Brown (*Primitive Constellations* I p. 338) states, 'The ecliptic was regarded as a "Yoke" laid across heaven and as "The Furrow of heaven" and in the

process of time this name of the ecliptic became transferred, as a technical term to Aldebaran.' It is at this star
(a Tauri) that the Somerset Hercules gazes along his sight
line from Antares in Scorpio to Aldebaran, the position of
which is marked at Hurst by a very distinct Kabalistic
symbol under the muzzle of the Bull and supported on his
hoof.[1]

It is this star that marked the commencement of the first
calendar at the vernal equinox, which nowadays is used so
much by astronomers to test their spectrographs. They
know its velocity very accurately, for it is receding from us
about 33 miles per second. On our modern planisphere
Aldebaran's place is in line with May 30th, but that is 69
degrees behind our equinox of today, or roughly 4,700
years ago. Norman Lockyer says in *The Dawn of Astronomy*, 'The Euphrates and Tigris rise at the Spring
Equinox — the religion was equinoctial, the temples were
directed to the east. The Nile rises at the Solstice — the
religion was solstitial and the solar temples were directed
no longer to the east.' But on those two words 'no longer'
hang the crux of the matter.

After the 'Ancient Empire' the Egyptian temples were
solstitial, but before the period of the Middle Kingdom they
were equinoctial. This points, according to Lockyer, to a
Babylonian intrusion of religious belief previous to 2000
B.C. He says, 'There was undoubtedly an equinox-
worshiping, pyramid-building race existing in Babylonia
at the time the Egyptian pyramids are supposed to have
been built. . . . We find ourselves then, in the presence of the
worship of the sun and stars in the ecliptic constellations
in Egypt during pyramid times, and in constellations
connected with the Equinox; for if we are right about the
Pleiades and Antares, these are the stars which heralded
the sunrise at the Vernal and Autumnal Equinox respectively, when the sun was in Taurus and Scorpio.'

According to Maspero, after many conflicts between
races of the north and south of Egypt, 'east and west
pyramid building practically ceased; Memphis takes
second place and Thebes comes upon the scene as the seat
of the XII Dynasty'.

So equinoctial worship is the link which astronomically

and mythologically connected the Nile Delta with Babylonia and Babylonia with Somerset. 'The Long Barrows of England are almost always placed with their long diameter east and west, while the primary interment is generally at the east end, which is broader and higher than the other.'

In this English zodiac it is not only the Sun god Hercules who looks due west, but the Goat, Water Carrier, both Fish, the Ram, the Twin, the Virgin and the Dragon's head; obviously no chance arrangement, but shows consummate genius in a ten-mile-wide sculpture on strictly geometrical lines converging to the centre. The Dragon's head lies at one apex of an imaginary central triangle, on the equinoctial line connecting Aldebaran and Antares. On it fall the stars of the Little Bear when transferred from the planisphere of the Northern Hemisphere to the map of the effigies.

This model of the star constellations was definitely a Solar Calendar, the solar year being the period of time in which the earth performs a revolution in its orbit about the sun, or passes from any point of the ecliptic (i.e. the circular path of the sun through the signs of the zodiac) to the same point again.

The solar day, the solar year of 365 days and the lunar month may be called the natural divisions of time. But as the lunar year has only 354 days this discrepancy between solar and lunar years has caused endless confusion all down the ages chiefly in connection with religious festivals. For instance, in the second century of our era, great disputes arose among the Christians respecting the proper time to celebrate Easter which governs all their other movable feasts; it was eventually fixed to take place on the Sunday which immediately follows the full moon that happens upon, or next after, the day of the vernal equinox, 21 March.

Julius Caesar abolished the use of the lunar year with its intercalary month, when the sun entered the sign Aries at the vernal equinox on 25 March, but strange to say we still, after two thousand years, cling to 21 March as the date when 'the Sun enters the sign Aries (Equinox)'; the sign, but *not* the constellation Aries, for it has advanced 30 degrees or the entire breadth of a zodiacal sign since Julius Caesar's time. This is so important to our subject that it is worth quoting from the Encyclopaedia Britannica in order to correct a generally accepted misunderstanding as to when the Sun enters the constellation Aries.

The signs are geometrical divisions 30 degrees in extent, counted from the Spring equinox in the direction of the sun's progress through them. The whole series accordingly shifts westwards through the effect of precession by about one degree in seventy-two years. At the moment of crossing the equator towards the north, the sun is said to be at the first point of Aries; some thirty days later it enters Taurus, and so on through Gemini, etc. The constellations bearing the same names coincided approximately in position, when Hipparchus observed them in Rhodes, with the divisions they designated. The discrepancy now, however, amounts to the entire breadth of a sign, the sun's path in Aries lying among the stars of Pisces, in Taurus among those of Aries, etc., etc.

'The Astrologers of today still use the signs, and ignore the constellations, which are where the stars really are', so can one be surprised when their prophecies do not come true?

If we apply the above statement to the Somerset lay-out of the constellations, we find that at this very date the sun is leaving the tail of the effigy Fish on Fishers Hill which leads to Wearyall Hill and is about to enter the tail of the Phoenix Water Carrier to climb Glastonbury Tor, slowly passing from the water to the air sign.

What the Phoenix will bring forth in her anguish during the next two thousand years that the sun inhabits its sacred precincts time only will prove. Can the fine old Abbey be restored in which to worship the Great Architect of the Universe? Can the little town of Glaston be cleansed by the waters of its once holy 'Chalice Well' (the Aquarius Cup) from the miasma of pseudo-occultism? Can it, by strictly scientific investigation of the ancient Wisdom, rise on the wings of this 'Evangelistic Eagle', soaring into the gold and azure of a new sunrise, the clouds of which are even now like a furnace of molten copper.

Up, up the long, delirious, burning blue
Where never lark, nor even eagle flew

'Behold the day cometh, that shall burn as an oven.... But unto you that fear my name shall the Sun of righteousness arise with healing in His wings.'

Malachi iv, 2.

4. THE ORIGIN OF THE STAR CONSTELLATIONS

Madame Blavatsky says (*Secret Doctrine* p. 502), 'As above so below. Sidereal phenomena, and the behaviour of the celestial bodies in the heavens, were taken as a model, and the plan was carried out below on earth. In the same manner and on the plan of the Zodiac in the upper Ocean or the heavens, a certain realm on Earth, an inland sea, was consecrated and called "the Abyss of Learning"; twelve centres on it in the shape of twelve small islands representing the Zodiacal signs — two of which remained for ages the "mystery signs" and were the abodes of twelve Heirophants and masters of wisdom. This "Sea of Knowledge" or learning remained for ages there.' May we suggest that the ancient Mystery School of Glastonbury's Holy Grail offers a parallel to the above.

The High History of the Holy Grail, translated by Dr. Sebastian Evans from the thirteenth century French original, gives us some interesting information about the Holy Grail (Branch XVIII Title 12). We are definitely told it existed at the time of the worship of the 'Bull of Copper'. (Taurus was worshipped from 4000 to 2000 B.C.) and that 'men with iron mallets' killed those that 'adore the bull' 1500 at one slaying.

We are also told that King Fisherman was dead, and 'his Priests' had vanished, but King Hermit (the chief Heirophant, uncle to Perceval) and twelve other hermits were still in the Kingdom. (Branch XXXV Title 15) 'He looketh and seeth on an island twelve hermits sitting on the seashore. They tell him that they have not far away twelve chapels and twelve houses that surround a graveyard wherein lie twelve dead knights that we keep watch over' (the twelve zodiacal signs?).

It is apparent that in 1888 when *The Secret Doctrine* was published it was known that the plan of the twelve zodiacal constellations had been laid out on earth in the form of a circular model, and, as in the Welsh legends, this replica of the heavens was regarded as 'the Abyss of

Learning' or 'sea of knowledge.'

To the question, 'Who made the Giant effigies of the Somerset Zodiac?' the answer would be the Sumer-Chaldeans. They were Astronomers, Astrologers and Priests. Originally from the coast of the Persian Gulf, they settled in Ur of the Chaldees and seized and held the region of old Sumer, the centre of the primitive non-Semitic culture which they adopted; a knowledge of the heavens was the very foundation of the system of belief unfolded by them. The lay-out of this zodiac was equinoctial, which characteristic hails from the Euphrates, and its vernal equinox that fixed the commencement of the year in Taurus was regulated by Marduk of Babylonia. Also it must have been laid out by a race that was familiar with the horse, bull, sheep, dog, etc., which were not indigenous to Egypt, but were in constant contact with the agricultural Sumer-Chaldeans at the date of the creation of these effigies about 2700 B.C. At the same time, as far as we know, no scorpions were to be found in England.

The English zodiac obviously belongs to an age of religion in its pristine simplicity and sincerity, when no symbols or ritualistic signs had crept in to mar its grandeur and extreme purity of expression. The thoughts of its creators apparently dwelt amongst the stars, reverently searching the heavens for revelations of divine wisdom.

The creatures depicted in the constellations were considered by the early Chaldeans as emanations of the Unfathomable One, like man himself; their names were as follows, and can be equated with the Knights of the Round Table headed by King Arthur and King Fisherman:

Ana— 'The Lord of the Earth' and 'House of Heaven.'

Ea— 'The Lord of the Deep,' 'The Fish Man.'

Bel— Senior of the gods in point of 'Time.'

Chaldean Hur— Sin 'The god thirty' as measuring the Moon month, 'The Architect.'

Twin to Hur— Ninda— 'The Setting Sun'. 'The keeper of hidden treasure.'

Shamsah— 'The Lord of Fire' and 'The House of the Sun

Raman— 'The Lord of the Air,' of fruitfulness, of canals

and rain.

Ishtar—The greatest goddess.

Nebo— 'The messenger of the gods,' special patron of astronomy.

Nergal—'The warrior god.'

The Sumer-Chaldeans were essentially clay modellers, and the earthwork giants of Somerset, which must be the oldest colossal relief modelling in the world, are in the realistic style of the early Babylonian seal cylinder impressions and not stylized or adorned as they would have been by Egyptians or Assyrians whose medium of expression was stone.

The fertilization of the giant effigies by a system of irrigation which even to this day is most elaborate, also points to the designers being agricultural water folk.

The Chaldean name Hur as a place-name alongside the Bull and Ship suggests the same conclusion, because he sits in his Chaldean symbol, a boat; and Khaldi in the Berber dialect designates the exact equivalent of Hur, which was the proper name of the Moon-god, the Chaldeans being Moon worshippers, before Gilgamesh rearranged the symbolic creatures as a zodiac.

The aborigines of South Wales, Cornwall and the Severn Valley — where the Zodiacal Circle lies — were the early 'Kelts', calling themselves 'Khaldis' or the early 'Chaldees', now universally known as of the Iberian Mediterranean and River-bed Type, having the long narrow skull, long face, dark hair and eyes of the long barrow builders, who were said to own the Magic Oracle Bowl or Cauldron of Wisdom; the Druids belonged to this race. There must have been thousands of inhabitants in Britain before 2,000 B.C. to enable the architect astrologers to construct the enormous earthworks and boundaries of the Giant effigies.

Lenormant, Jensen and Epping have all traced the traditional zodiacal constellations to the Chaldeans; and Dr. Waddell has fully demonstrated the kinship between the Sumerian, Babylonian and aboriginal British stock, in his well-illustrated *British Edda*. He points out that their respective monuments testify to the Edda being the joint national epic regarding King Arthur, the Holy Grail, the Giants and Eden.

The poets and historians of the Greeks, Goths, Persians, Indians, Finns, Britons and even Greenlanders, upon almost every occasion describe these giants so much alike, that it is evident they all drew from one original and that their models are copied from nature. This remarkable concurrence of evidence from times and places so remote from each other carries all the force of truth; the Greeks complimented the Kelts on their descent from the Giants, but no other race claim kinship with them.

A well-known fact is that Nimrod, who has been identified with Marduk, Gilgamesh and Orion, was called the 'great Titan and Giant'. Being a sun worshipper, he is said to have taken the famous 'Cauldron' from the moon worshippers in the early Bronze Age.

We have often been told that astronomy is found in a developed form among the ancient Babylonians, traceable back to 3,000 B.C., but not until I discovered this 'Temple of the Stars' in Somerset in A.D. 1,925 and photographed it from the air, have we been able to define exactly the original features forming the zodiac.

It was known that by 2,250 B.C. the combination of prominent groups of stars with outlines of pictures had been put together to form a zodiac; and 'the theory of the ecliptic as representing the course of the sun through the year, divided among twelve constellations with a measurement of 30 degrees to each division, was also of Babylonian origin, as has now been definitely proved'
(*Encyclopaedia Britannica*).

'Chaldean wisdom' became in the classical world the synonym of this science of astronomy which in its character was so essentially religious. For thousands of years it appears to have kept this sacred character in the traditions of the Holy Grail, the Quest of which so closely resembles the adventures of Gilgamesh, the Sumerian.

Gilgamesh or Marduk or Nimrod

Thanks to Layard's discovery of the library of the Temple of Nebo at Nineveh, the British Museum possesses two very early records of the creation of the zodiacal giants. They are *The Epic of Gilgamesh King of Erech,* called 'He who hath seen all things', and *The Babylonian Legend of the Creation.*

Briefly the story is as follows: Gilgamesh possessed all knowledge and wisdom and travelled far over sea and land, but to thwart him a goddess 'washed her hands, took a piece of clay, cast it upon the ground and made a male creature' called Enkidu. (A satyr found sporting with fishes, Capricornus.)

Though he was mighty in stature and strength he could not kill Gilgamesh, and they became great friends; they went together to fight the fire-breathing giant Khumbaba, whose head, with the help of the Sun god, Gilgamesh cut off.

The inference is that he is acting the same part as King Arthur who also cut off the head of this giant spit-fire (Draco).

The goddess Ishtar (Virgo) then makes love to Gilgamesh, but he tells her that every creature falling under her sway suffered mutilation or death, so in revenge she had Taurus — 'the heavenly Bull with enormous horns' — created, but he too was unable to kill Gilgamesh, and the bull's heart or horns were offered to the Sun god.

Then Enkidu met a monster 'with Lion's claws'. Leo attacked him and led him away to the Under World, and here is the anguished turning point of the epic, for Gilgamesh laments thus:

My friend whom I loved hath become like the dust.
Enkidu, my friend whom I loved hath become like dust.
Shall not I myself also be obliged to lay me down
And never again rise up to all eternity?

So to find the Heaven of the dead Gilgamesh set out for the west, and came to the mountain where the sun was said to 'both rise and set'. It was guarded by Scorpio, 'the Scorpion man' whose glance killed mortals; he told him it took twelve double hours to traverse the mountain.

Nothing daunted, having passed through the hours of darkness, he finds the 'tree of the gods' in a lovely garden where the Sun god spoke to him. 'The trees were laden with precious stones instead of fruit.'

Here we find that universal tree in the garden, Ygdrasil the Cosmic Tree, with stars for fruit, that grows in Paradise, that ancestral abode of the old Chaldeans for

which they preserved so distinct and reverent a conception, calling it Arallu, the Land of the Dead, where is 'the
pillar around which the heavenly spheres revolve'.

On coming to the shore of a vast sea our hero is told:

'The Waters of Death which bar its front are deep.

If then, Gilgamesh, thou art able to cross the sea,

When thou arrivest at the Waters of Death what wilt
thou do?

Just as Gilgamesh saw the shores of the island of
Khasisadra and returned from them strong and healthy,
after his sores were washed in a fountain of healing
waters, so we find thousands of other pilgrims dared the
dangers of desert and ocean to bathe in the Chalice Blood
Spring at Glastonbury. Even his ancestors at the time of
the Flood had already crossed the sea in a giant boat,
which boat now awaited him.

Gilgamesh said unto him, to Uta-Napishtim the remote:

I am looking at thee, Uta-Napishtim.

At rest thou dost lie upon thy back.

How then hast thou stood the company of the gods?

After relating the story of the Deluge and the building of
his boat, his ancestor says:

I will reveal unto thee, Gilgamesh, a hidden mystery,

And a secret matter of the gods I will declare unto thee.

Then he told him of the old city on the River Parutti (see
Parrett river guarding the sacred area) where the star gods
dwell, and asked him this question: 'Now as touching
thyself; who will gather the gods together for thee, so that
thou mayest find the life which thou seekest?'

That question seems to have been answered in the
Babylonian Legend of the Creation, for Marduk gathered
together all the eleven allies of Tiamat in his net, who were
the twelve constellation giants of the zodiac. And he took
the 'Tablet of Destinies' from Kingu's 'breast, sealed it
with his seal and put it on his own breast' and he devised
a 'cunning plan'.

It appears that the Sumerian ruler, in converting the
early Chaldean Moon calendar to that of the Sun, set in
order and restored the original giant effigies of the 'abode
of Ea'. In any case we are told, he determined to carry out
a series of works of creation by forming the dome of

heaven and its reverse, which latter was put 'over against the deep'; he thus became the 'celestial architect'. He founded E-Sharra, 'which he made to be heaven', and 'a microcosm in which man was to do service to the gods'.

Unfortunately the text of the Fifth Tablet is missing; when it is found it may throw light on this point. Undoubtedly it would have supplied details as to Marduk's arrangement and regulations for the Sun, the Moon, the stars and the signs of the zodiac. But we are told:

'He crossed heaven, he contemplated the regions thereof.

He betook himself to the abode of Ea that is opposite the Deep.

The Lord Marduk measured the dimensions of the Deep,

He appointed the Stations for the great gods,

He set in heaven the Stars of the Zodiac which are their likeness.

He fixed the year, he appointed the limits thereof.

He fixed the zenith in the heavenly vault.

The gods, his fathers, looked on the net which he had made.

They observed how craftily the bow had been constructed.'

Let these words be heard without ceasing, may they reign to all eternity,

Because he made the heavenly places and moulded the stable earth.

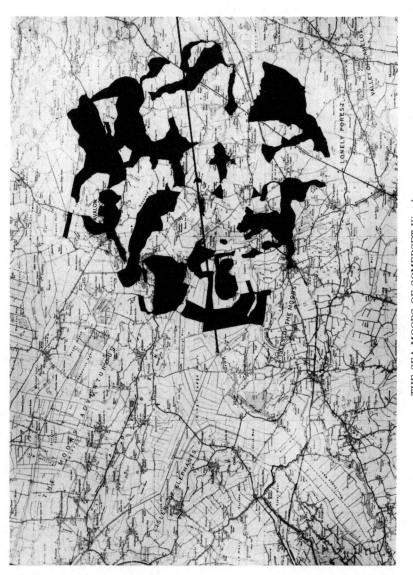

THE SEA MOORS OF SOMERSET: Kingdom
of Logres

5. *ZODIACAL GIANTS*

There are records of Initiates from Egypt travelling in a northwesterly direction, with the object of building 'colossal Zodiacs', their destination being the British Isles (*Secret Doctrine* II). Let it be remembered however, that the Dolmen and Menhir builders 'in stone' belong to a different race from the modellers in clay, who were river-bed men like the Ohio and Mississippi valley Mound Builders. As I have pointed out, the Babylonian clay tablets record that the goddess 'took a piece of CLAY, cast it upon the ground, and made a male creature'.

But the interesting fact remains that this time Blavatsky traces records of the building of a British zodiac, as coming from Egypt, whereas 'the Zodiacal Ring on Earth' which she describes (p. 502), with twelve little islands set in an inland sea, hails from Asia. The latter exactly pictures the 'Temple of the Stars', in England, for the signs are set in what are called on the map, the Sea Moors. The low-lying land has now been more or less drained, but in winter time the little hills appear as islands emerging from the flooded Sea Moors. Probably the 'Initiates' came via Egypt, to lay out this zodiac.[1]   Now as to that layout, each 'little island' in this 'Abyss of Learning' takes the form of a zodiacal Giant.

The *Secret Doctrine* states (p. 277), 'Of Giants who were in the earth in those days of old, the Bible alone had spoken to the wise men of the West, the Zodiac being the solitary witness called upon to corroborate the statement in the person of Atlas or Orion, whose mighty shoulders are said to support the World.'

In *A Guide to Glastonbury's Temple of the Stars* there is a chapter devoted to the Giant Orion, illustrated by an Ordnance Survey Map of his effigy, and a fine air view photo in the Supplement showing his head and shoulders and upraised right arm, in the form of a square, so there is no necessity to repeat here the facts concerning that effigy and its significance. He was certainly one of the three famous Giants imprisoned in the circle of the god TIME, of which Hesiod tells in the War of the Giants.

Here they sit, Age after Age in melancholy state,
Still pining in eternal gloom, and lost to every comfort,
Round them wide extend the dreary bounds of earth, and
    sea,
And air of heaven above, and Tartarus below.

Hesiod's date was 907 B.C., and on the sculptured constellations in the National Museum at Naples, called the Farnese Globe, of 72 B.C., the path of the Sun is shown passing through the Giant Orion's fingers as it does in the Somerset original, for he was once one of the Twins. A photo of this valuable antiquarian classic is in Basil Brown's illustrated *Astronomical Atlases, Maps and Charts*.

Lucian, the Greek, tells us that 'in the battle between the gods and giants the gods took the form of animals', meaning the giant zodiacal animals, called in Babylonia the Star gods. A paraphrased version of the old lines may serve as a reminder of their order as we now know it:

The Ram, the Bull, the Heavenly Twins,
And next to them the Lion stands,
The Virgin and the Scorpion clawed,
The Archer Hercules, and Goat,
The bird that bears the Water-pot,
And two Fish tied on to the Whale.

Besides Orion, the other two Giants in human form depicted in the Somerset earthworks are Virgo and Hercules. The Virgin it has been said 'began as Queen of Heaven and ended as witch'. As a matter of fact her metamorphoses have been countless, but we hope history will never lose sight of the fact that her first 'Kern-Baby' was a wheat sheaf plucked from Wheat-hill.

This 'Archer' Hercules was also a 'Vegetation god' when he first fell from heaven; and quite unwittingly the country folk, living on his tilled acres, still eat the body and drink the blood of a god, whereas, less than two thousand years ago their forebears, knowingly, partook of them in all sincerity. In Holland the genius of fertility was represented by a pair of giants that were taken about the fields in the procession of Corpus Christi, up till A.D. 1745

and, as Gog and Magog, two colossal statues stood in the
Guild Hall, London, the legend being that these Giants
were the survivors of those taken by Bruit of Troy when he
came to England and founded the city of London, calling it
New Troy. He was celebrated in the Welsh Triads as one of
the 'Three King Revolutionists of Britain' about 1000 B.C.
Lord Chief Justice Cope affirmed, 'the original laws of
this land were composed of such elements as Brutus first
selected from the Ancient Greek and Trojan institutions'.

The Royal Primogeniture, by which the succession to the
Throne of Britain was vested in the eldest son or daughter
of the King, was known as the 'Trojan law'. Another
memory of their colonization is perpetuated in the Mazes
cut in the turf in all parts of England and Wales, called the
'Walls of Troy' or Welsh shepherd's 'Troy Towns'.

This passion for carving history on Britain's hills is
exemplified in Uffington's White Horse, measuring 335
feet long by 120 feet, the Cern Abbas Hercules, and
Wilmington Giant. But the Somerset Giants, besides being
drawn in outline like the above, are much larger and in
part carved and modelled. They are scientifically laid out
in a circle whereas the others are solitary; but above all
they correspond with the stars of their respective constellations in the sky.

In London, the giants Gog and Magog used to 'stalk
before my Lord Mayor's Pageants' on St. John's eve. They
were housed at the Guild Hall in Charles II's reign in 1666;
fresh ones were made in 1708. 'And thus attended by his
direful dog. The gyant was (God bless us) Gog-magog.'

Giants were a part of the pageantry used in different
cities of England. For the festival of St. John Baptist in
1564, Chester brought out four giants, with animals,
besides hobby horses, but the Mayor of Chester caused
them 'to be broken, and not to goe the Devil in his
feathers'.

At the points of the compass of this 'Zodiacal Ring on
Earth' lie the four so called 'Evangelistic symbols'; the
east corresponds with the Man, St. Matthew, because if a
line be projected from the centre it passes through the eye
of Hercules, due east; the south with the Lion, St. Mark,
the line passing through Leo, due south; the west with the

Bull, St. Luke, the line passing through the eye of Taurus, due West; and the north with the Bird, St. John, the line passing through the Phoenix of this Zodiac, due north. Many thousands of times the 'Evangelists' have been represented thus in Christian Art. We now know they date back to what archaeologists call 'the early Bronze Age' marking the actual foundations of 'the First Church in Britain', as has always been maintained! Apparently history may err but legend seldom; the memory of the race survives.

Passing round the circle of Giants the enormous Scorpion, lying between Hercules and Virgo, bars the Fosse Way; he has been the symbol of death from early Babylonian days and can be seen represented on the boundary stone of Nebuchadnezzar I, of 1,120 B.C., in the British Museum. The Mythraic sculptures of the Roman period found in England also depict him; it was at that time his claws were converted into the sign of the Scales in which, metaphorically, to weigh the souls of the departed.

There remain to be mentioned the constellations of the Ram, the Fish, the Water Pot, and the Goat; the latter's gigantic horn, 'Cornucopia, is a Masonic emblem, and corroborates the fact that the major part of masonic symbols has an astronomical significance'.[2] In point of time they are much nearer to us than the other signs, the Ram reigning supreme for the two thousand years and more before our era; consequently, we read in the New Testament of 'The Lamb slain for the foundation of the World', 'The throne of God and of the Lamb', and 'These are they which follow the Lamb ... being the first fruits unto God and to the Lamb.'

It is accordingly interesting to see that, as in the Persian Zodiac, it is the outline of a Lamb and not a Ram that lies on the slope of the hill opposite to the great Fish effigy near Glastonbury.

Jesus Christ ushered in the water sign Pisces in our year One, and baptism by water (instead of fire as in the preceding Fire Sign Aries), hence the legend that He landed, as a child, with Joseph of Arimathea on Wearyall Hill which forms the Fish.

It is a remarkable fact that the Whale, in all modern

pictures of the stars, is shown tied on to the two fish, as in this Somerset original; and that the Arthurian legends make so much of the bridges that connect them as well as of the king of the Castle of the Whale. During the two thousand years of this Water Sign, men have gone down to the sea in ships and done business in the great waters; but as the Sun is about to pass into the Air Sign Aquarius, at the spring equinox, what do we see? Flight has taken the place of ships.

Did the cosmographers who chose so remote a site upon which to lay out the model of the zodiac nearly five thousand years ago foresee that at this exact juncture in human history the whole world would be baptized in blood, and so chose a natural spring turning blood red the stone over which it flows and a solitary lofty hill, carved in the form of a Phoenix, as the only fitting symbols for an age of rebirth and regeneration? If so, this zodiac was indeed worthily called of old the 'Cauldron of Wisdom' for from Glastonbury's Tor the Phoenix, with outstretched wings, rising towards the Sun-rise, has drunk deep of the Cup of Blood — Chalice Blood Spring it is named on the map — but, self consuming and self renewing, it was a 'symbol of a secret cycle and Initiation' to the Hebrews as well as the Egyptians.

6. THE FINGER OF THE LAW IN BRITAIN'S ZODIAC

Ra spake, 'Let there be set a field,' and there appeared the Field of Rest, 'Therein do I gather as its inhabitants, things which hang from heaven, even the stars.' There is one feature in the British Zodiac that is not represented as far as I know in any of its copies, and that is the outline of a great finger at the exact intersection of imaginary crosslines connecting the four famous Royal Stars, Regulus, Aldebaran, Fomalhaut and Antares; it seems to be the chief proof that Egyptian influence was at work here. The finger can be seen on the second illustration.

When the Israelites had been brought forth out of the land of Egypt, the Bible tells us in two separate books, Exodus and Deuteronomy, the tables of the Law given to Moses on Mount Sinai were 'written with the finger of God'; in both instances this statement is followed by the account of the making of the golden calf to which was offered burnt offerings. The expression 'the finger of God' was an Egyptian figure of speech, a symbol of inexorable law; it was used by the magicians in speaking to Pharoah in reference to the plagues of Egypt when they confessed, 'this is the finger of God'.

One of the latest scientific theories is that memory is indestructible, and the discovery in Somerset proves that for 4,700 years this finger has been remembered as the symbol of God's laws, as uncompromising as those of mathematics.

Cosmic energy is based upon mathematical sequence; the ancients knew that it was only on these lines that the seeker could find his way out of nebulous kind of thought, for Law is *one* throughout and it can always be trusted to lead us on to further knowledge.

Consequently, in laying out the 'Temple of the Stars' in England it was this great finger outlined upon the earth that was made to point into the eye of Taurus, thus indicating for all time the date of the temple equinox. And just as in Exodus and Deuteronomy the finger and the

golden calf are associated, so here in Somerset the Bull
was worshipped, for *The High History of the Holy Grail*
says, 'And he [Perceval] entereth into the castle, where he
findeth within great plenty of folk that all were mis-
believers and of feeble belief. He seeth the bull of copper in
the midst of the castle right big and horrible, that was
surrounded on all sides by folk that all did worship
thereunto together round about. So intent were they upon
adoring the bull that, an any had been minded to slay
them what time they were yet worshipping the same, they
would have allowed him so to do, and would have thought
that they were saved thereby, and save this had they none
other belief in the world' (Branch 18 Titles 11-12). And in
the Bible Moses says, 'So I turned and came down from
the mount, and the mount burned with fire, and the two
tables of the covenant were in my two hands. And I
looked, and, behold ye had sinned against the Lord your
God, and had made you a molten calf.'

Now these tables of the covenant are the ones that were
'written with the finger of God', so this connection is not
merely a coincidence but throws a valuable side light on
the minds of those early Egyptian Initiates who collab-
orated in building the 'colossal zodiac'; they must have
believed that God's Universal Laws were, as the New
Testament says, able to cast out devils, 'But if I, by the
finger of God cast out devils, then is the kingdom of God
come upon you.' Those of 'feeble belief' still mistakenly
worship what they do not understand; theirs is the fault
not the law, for the calf or bull 'Taurus' is only one of the
immemorial symbols of the Universe around us, and it was
when the Sun was in this sign at the spring equinox that
the chart of the stars is known to have been designed.[1]

The original effigy symbols speak for themselves with a
forceful language of their own which the modern copies
have completely lost, though using the same constellation
figures. They show us why and how the temple was laid
out, the traditions of which Freemasons have kept, for in
Operative Masonry the Egyptian method of surveying and
orientation is the Guild method still in use. They first find
the central line by running a blue cord or handline from
the position of the Sun's rising above the horizon to the

Holy Place, i.e. from east to west. Upon and from the centre line given by the Sun, the masons fixed the centre and the four corners of the intended Temple. In the Egyptian Underworld there are 'twelve bearers of cord' whose function is to measure; the cord we are told is the 'cord of law' and it is upon the cord of the 'centre line' that the great Finger lies in Somerset, pointing to Taurus.

The branch of the Egyptian priesthood 4,000 years ago and more, whose work was surveying, was called 'Cord-Stretchers'. A religious ceremony 'the stretching of the cord' was held to fix the axis and orientation, and the priest 'read the sacred text during the laying of the foundation stone and during the fixing of the four corners with accuracy by the four supports of heaven'.

Many years ago the Lord of the Manor of Butleigh, where the finger lies, told me that it was the custom in olden times for people of the West Country to express the wish in their wills to be buried in 'The Most Holy Grave', meaning Butleigh; he never knew that the village occupies the very heart of the sacred area, and that there are three enclosures on his land of equal interest, the three points of the central triangle. But it is evident that the memory of the sacredness of his village was still alive up to comparatively recent times. (My *Guide* illustrates all three enclosures.)

It is remarkable that this finger symbolizing Law should be woven into the Coronation Ceremony of the Kings of England, and proves that the Church knew its archaic significance, for during the coronation the Archbishop places a ring on the King's finger. Much of the ritual accompanying the reception of the ring has now been omitted — the coronation of James I, 1603, was the last time that this remnant of ceremonial magic was performed, but part of the 'Exorcism' ran thus, 'God the creator of all things in heaven and earth, the ffownteyne of spiritual grace, which doest write thy laws in the harts of the ffaithful with thyne own finger, to whom the Egiptian Sorcerers yeelding confessed this is the "finger of God." '

Here again the finger is associated with God's laws which the King, now invested with 'the wedding ring of England', is pledged to support. The ring itself is an echo of the single ruby of the Grail, for by tradition it should be a plain gold ring with a large table ruby on which is engraved a plain St. George's cross — it never leaves the person of the King.

Shakespeare, as well as the Church, knew the tradition regarding Eden and Paradise, 'Paradise Garden, that thing which men call "the Grail", for in the dying words of old Gaunt he says:

This royal throne of kings, this sceptred isle,
This earth of majesty, this seat of Mars,
This other Eden, demi-paradise...
This blessed plot, this earth, this realm, this England.

Mars was originally a 'Sun god, a god of wind and storm, a god of the year, and a god of vegetation'.

The more one studies 'this colossal zodiac' the more one is impressed by the conviction that, as Herbert Spencer puts it in his *Education*:

Devotion to science is a tacit worship — a tacit recognition of worth in the things studied, and by implication in their Cause. It is not a mere lip-homage, but a homage expressed in action — not a mere professed respect, but a respect proved by the sacrifice of time, thought and labour.

It is religious, too, inasmuch as it generates a profound respect for, and an implicit faith in, those uniform Laws which underlie all things. By accumulated experiences the man of science acquires a thorough belief in the unchanging relations of phenomena — in the invariable connection of cause and consequence — in the necessity of good or evil results. Instead of the rewards and punishments of traditional belief, which men vaguely hope they may gain, or escape, in spite of their disobedience; he finds that there are rewards and punishments in the ordained constitution of things, and that the evil results of disobedience are inevitable. He sees that the Laws to which we must submit are not only inexorable but beneficent. He sees that in virtue of these Laws, the process of things is ever towards a greater perfection and a higher happiness. Hence he is led constantly to insist on these laws, and is indignant when men disregard them. And thus does he, by asserting the eternal principles of things and the necessity of conforming to them, prove himself intrinsically religious.

To all this add the further religious aspect of science, that it alone can give us true conception of ourselves and our relation to the mysteries of existence. It realizes to us in a way which nothing else can, the littleness of human intelligence in the face of that which transcends human intelligence.'

Then straightway lay thy dexter finger on thy lips and say:

O Silence! Silence! Silence!
The Symbol of the Living God beyond decay.

Mithraic Ritual

PART II

INTRODUCTION

King Arthur's Round Table or the Grail[1]

King Arthur's Round Table was not just a piece of
furniture as might be supposed but something vastly more
worthy upon which to found a Knightly Order; his table
was the Round Table of the Stars, of which fuller
information is given in my *Guide to Glastonbury's Temple
of the Stars*. This design was found laid out on the ground
near Glastonbury, and is 30 miles in circumference, the
earthworks which form it were constructed by the Early
Bronze Age inhabitants; it constitutes a sculptural relief of
unequalled magnitude. The outlines of the figures have
been traced from the maps of the districts where the giant
effigies lie. The Creatures represent the envisaged star
constellations of 5,000 years ago and, as we shall see, our
present solar calendar is founded upon this design.

The Giant figures are — The Scorpion, Archer, Goat,
Water-Carrier, Fishes, young Ram, Bull, Twins, Lion and
Virgin.

If the modern planisphere be placed upon this map, it
will be found that the stars of the corresponding constellations fall into their own effigies. The skill of this circular
composition, which was made to fit the stars round the
dome of the sky, partly lies in its contraction towards the
central point, or zenith of the celestil sphere, from which
these twelve zodiacal divisions radiate.

SIGNS AND SECRETS 1: *Aquarius*

King Arthur's remains were said to have been buried in a tomb richly carved with lions and placed in the Choir of Glastonbury Abbey in front of the high altar, but about A.D. 1130 the Norman monks William of Malmesbury and John of Glaston saw the two Pyramids in the Abbey precincts between which he lay originally.[1]

The Abbey grounds lie directly under the imaginary ecliptic drawn by a dotted line on the illustration shown in the frontispiece. This path of the sun shows clearly how the first zodiacal design was dependent upon it and is a sure proof of accurate observation of the stars, the date that corresponds on the modern planisphere being 17 March or the end of the Babylonian year; the ancient Roman year also commenced in March.

This date, strange to say, is St. Patrick's Day; he died A.D. 472, and William of Malmesbury tells us, 'when the Old Church was burned his body was gathered into a Pyramid, beside the Altar towards the south, which out of veneration for the Saint was afterwards nobly clothed in gold and silver'.

But why another Pyramid? The pyramid tomb was a solar symbol of the highest sacredness as at Heliopolis 'a symbol upon which, from the day when he created the gods, the Sun-god was accustomed to manifest himself in the form of the Phoenix', as on the polished apex of the Dahshur pyramid we still see a winged sun disk surmounting a pair of eyes which face east.

These Glastonbury Abbey pyramids were undoubtedly carrying on the tradition of the great earthwork pyramid of the Isle of Avalon, which, if seen from the hills of the surrounding neighbourhood, is breath-taking in its appeal to the imagination, as it rears itself out of the Hyperborean mists of the Sea Moors and takes the form of the effigy Phoenix, the manifestation of the Sun-god.

Thus Glaston Tor, crowned by St. Michael's tower on the high altar of the Sun-god, really stands for King Arthur's grave. The first monks knew the secret of his passing in

1,130 as demonstrated by the two pyramids, one 28 feet high and the other 26 feet high.

So we can now understand the 'sage high Merlin' when he said 'that Arthur should yet come to help the English for the British believe yet that he is alive, and dwelling in Avalun and the British ever yet expect when Arthur shall return.'[2]

The last words of Tennyson's *Passing of Arthur* are 'And the new sun rose bringing the new year.'

During the winter, the sun was thought to rest in this northern-most effigy, which represents the constellation Aquarius, here the 'Evangelistic symbol' of the bird. It is represented on the Abbey tithe barn with the bull, lion and man.

This Glastonbury Phoenix might be compared to the mythical bird of India, Garuda, for it carries the cup of regeneration or ambrosia, whose therapeutic waters rise in Glaston's Tor and fill the aquarius pot called Chalice Blood Well, whilst spread out below lies his 'Wheel of Time' or Chakra.

Again, the Assyrian god Assur and the Median god Ahura Mazda are generally depicted with wings of the divine bird extended behind them and the circle of the sun's path surrounding them; on the standard of Sargon II, King of Assyria, we see the Bull, Lion, Archer and great Water-pot from which the stream of life issues, the Archer being the sun-god Assur, whereas on the Glastonbury zodiac, Hercules (or King Arthur) riding the horse of the Archer is the sun-god.

In Java the constellation of Aquarius is represented only by the great Water-pot and Pisces only by the Whale. The Whale on the Somerset planisphere lies just below the Phoenix that towers above it, spilling its once miraculous waters under the whale's tail, which connects the two fish of Pisces.

As at the centre of this zodiac a 'crown' or 'Mitre' is figured enclosing Draco's head,[3] we must not forget the Chaldean bird Zu which E.M. Plunket points out as representing Aquarius, in her *Ancient Calendars and Constellations*. Zu forced his way at an early hour into the chamber of destiny before the sun had risen and perceived within it the royal insignia of Bell, 'the Mitre of his power, the garment of his divinity — the fatal tablets of his divinity, Zu perceived them. He perceived the father of the gods, the god that is the tie between heaven and earth' and Zu seized the tablets of fate. 'This misfortune had arisen only once, at the beginning of the ages' (Maspero *Dawn of Civilization*).

The Legend of the Aquarius bird seizing 'the tablets of fate' points to a Chaldean origin for this astrological lay-out of the Somerset effigies, which might be called a 'chamber of destiny'.

The photograph does not show that the crested head of the Phoenix is turned towards its tail in order to reach the Blood Spring, whilst its breast is 'turned towards the rays of the sun, by the flapping of its wings', but this can be seen in the frontispiece. To quote from the Latin bestiaries, 'It is a bird of Arabia and of a purple colour. It is single and unique. When it has reached the age of five hundred years it becomes conscious that it has grown old and thereupon proceeds to collect the twigs of aromatic plants, frankincense, myrrh and other spices, of which it con-structs for itself a funeral pile. Having mounted upon it and being turned towards the rays of the sun, by the flapping of its wings it fans into flames a fire for its own burning and burns itself up. But on the third day after, it rises as a new bird from its ashes. According to other texts the scene is laid in the City of Heliopolis where the priest of the temple, being apprised of its coming, prepares an altar on which it alights and burns itself up. The first day after its burning he comes and finds a little worm in the ashes which emits an "exceeding sweet smell"; the second day he finds it has assumed the form of a little bird, and on the third it has become full grown. Then it bids a polite farewell to the priest and flies away a full and perfect phoenix. (This phase is illustrated in Dr. Dyson Perrins' bestiary.) The story of the phoenix taught the lesson of the Resurrection.'

On Glastonbury Tor King Arthur's spirit still broods in the wings of the Phoenix that hover over the 'elixir of life' springing from the Blood Well.

Hone says in *Ancient Mysteries*, 'When Edward VI was

crowned king 1546, on his way to Westminster, a heaven
with sun and stars and clouds was shown to him; from
beams of gold a phoenix descended down to a mount of
sweet shrubs, and there sitting, a lion of gold crowned,
made amity to the phoenix. Also beside the throne, on
which a child was seated representing the king, was "the
golden fleece", kept by two bulls and a serpent, their
mouths flaming out fire.'

SIGNS AND SECRETS 2: *Pisces*

Keltic tradition held that 'the Salmon of Knowledge was the oldest living thing, whoso ate of him would enjoy all the wisdom of the ages'. He was said to haunt the Severn River. Only three miles up a tributary of the Severn stands Glastonbury, buttressed by its famous Wearyall Hill upon which Joseph of Arimathea landed. This hill for generations has been pointed out to visitors as 'the burial place of a gigantic sacred salmon', part of it being called Fisher's Hill. On the map and from the air Wearyall takes the shape of a salmon and in fact forms one of the effigy fish of the Somerset zodiac.

St. Joseph brought with him to this sacred hill two silver vessels containing 'blood and water which had flowed from the side of the dead Christ' or, as others state, the cup or dish of the Holy Grail. On this subject A.E. Waite wrote in connection with Robert de Barron's poem, 'As regards the Fish, by which there is brought to remembrance an early and pregnant form of Christian symbolism, the text offers a comparison which, although a little cryptic, seems also significant. It says that in sight of the Grail, in its presence and the service thereof, true believers experience as much satisfaction as a fish, which, having been taken by a man in his hand has contrived to escape therefrom and again go swimming in the sea. The specific Fish of the story was placed before the Sacred Vessel, as instructed, and was covered with a cloth. There is no suggestion that it was eaten, and it appears to have remained as a kind of fixed dish whenever the Service was celebrated' at Daily Mass.[1]

From such vague glimmerings out of an intentionally shrouded past scholars have tried to uncover the source of the Grail legends, but until the layout of the star gods was discovered in their neighbourhood they had no solid foundation upon which to work, for the Romans, with appalling barbarity, wiped out the priests of the ancient wisdom.

Joseph of Arimathea, however, barely standing on the threshold of Christianity — for it was he who laid the body of Jesus in his tomb[2] — knew little of the new religion that was to sweep away stellar theology and must have been steeped in old traditions, being a wealthy tin and lead trader. These circumstances may have prompted him to collect Christ's blood whilst hanging upon the symbolic cosmic cross, for here was the stupendous moment when the Sun was passing from the constellation Aries into that of Pisces, according to the precession of the equinoxes.

As prophesied, a new god had been born heralding a new age, and the human sacrifice had been made, in proof of which Joseph carried the blood from Jerusalem 'beyond the ocean to the isles called the Britannic Isles'[3] where lay the already 3,000 year old Calendar.

The book which was called The Holy Grail is said to have recorded that St. Joseph's company came over in 'a ship that was sent by the Lord which King Solomon had curiously wrought in his day to last till the time of Christ.'[4] Joseph must have known of the Chaldean allegory which told that the fish was a symbol of the 'resurrecting' sun which the Sumerians invoked for resurrection from the dead, for herein lies the profound secret teaching of the Holy Grail.

Layard, in his Nineveh and Babylon, gives illustrations of the fish-god that he found and says, 'Each entrance was formed of two colossal bas-reliefs of Dagon or the Fish-god.... We can scarcely hesitate to identify this mythic form with the Oannes, or sacred man-fish who issued from the Erythraean Sea, instructed the Chaldeans in all wisdom, in the sciences, and in the fine arts, and was afterwards worshipped as a god in the temples of Babylonia.' Here we find the direct progenitor of the Keltic 'Salmon of Knowledge'.

But Joseph of Arimathea had by no means finished his mission by laying the sacred blood on the altar of the fish; the wooden peg must be stuck in the Calendar — as was the custom with primitive calendars — and to this day cuttings from Joseph's staff that he planted in Wearyall Hill, known as the Holy Thorn of Glastonbury, still flourish in all parts of the world.

Having thus marked the spot for the new spring
equinox, he established the British Church by settling the
'twelve disciples'[5] in the Isle of Avalon. William of
Malmesbury's *Antiquities of Glastonbury* states, 'And
thus, many succeeding these — but always twelve in
number — abode in the said island during many years, up
to the coming of St. Patric, the Apostle of the Irish.'

In view of the new evidence of the Somerset zodiac, it
was in token of the twelve 'signs' that the pagan kings
gave the 'Twelve Hides' of land to the twelve companions
accompanying Joseph, for again we read, 'But the
barbaric king and his people, hearing such novel and
unaccustomed things, absolutely refused to consent to
their preaching, neither did he wish to change the
tradition of his ancestors' (stellar theology or sun worship)
and 'at their request confirmed the twelve portions to
them after the heathen manner'.

To this day we can stand on the exact spot where Joseph
founded his church 'fashioning its walls below, circular-
wise'. Gildas, the British historian (A.D. 516-570), says
(Sec. 8): 'Meanwhile these islands ... received the beams of
light, that is, the Holy precepts of Christ, the true Sun ... at
the latter part, as we know, of the reign of Tiberius
Caesar.'

Avalon's island, with avidity
Claiming the death of pagans,
More than all in the world beside,
For the entombment of them all,
Honoured by chanting spheres of prophecy:
And for all time to come
Adorned shall it be
By them that praise the Highest.
Amid these Joseph in marble,
Of Arimathea by name,
Hath found perpetual sleep:
When his sarcophagus
Shall be found entire, intact,
In time to come, it shall be seen
And shall be open unto all the world.

                              Melkin, the British bard

The Golden Fleece[1] was placed in the Sacred Grove of
Aries, under the protection of the sleepless Dragon; in
Somerset the lamb 'Aries' has a golden fleece when its
well-tilled acres ripple with golden corn before harvest,
and it is guarded by Draco's head, at the centre of the
circle of zodiacal effigies.

It lies on high ground, in full sight of Glastonbury Tor
and is depicted with traditionally reverted head looking
west to the early British port on Bridgwater Bay. So
important is the turn of the head over the right shoulder
that it has been perpetuated on star maps and in the
Agnus Dei till the present day, combined with the bent
back foot and heavy tail. On Egypt's circular planisphere
from Dendera — now in Paris — Aries is shown with these
characteristics. The tail of this Somerset ram lamb, like
the Dendera one, suggests the broad-tailed species
common to Asia and Egypt, which often weighs 70 to 80
lbs.

The Ram is reckoned the first of the zodiacal signs.
Josephus declares it was when the sun was in Aries that
the Jewish people were delivered from the bondage of
Egypt. 'And the Lord spake unto Moses[2] and Aaron in the
land of Egypt, saying, This month shall be unto you the
beginning of months: it shall be the first month of the year
to you.... Then Moses called for the elders of Israel, and
said unto them, Draw out and take you a lamb according
to your families, and kill the passover. And ye shall take a
bunch of hissop, and dip it in the blood that is in the basin,
and strike the lintel and the two side posts with blood that
is in the basin ... the Lord will pass over the door, and will
not suffer the destroyer to come in unto your houses to
smite you' (Exodus xii).

The first symptom of the worship of the Lamb among
the Israelites is to be found in the substitution of the Ram
in the place of Isaac, by Abraham, for a sacrifice, and in
the New Testament we read, 'Behold the Lamb of God,
which taketh away the sins of the world,' 'The Lamb slain

from the foundation of the world'.

Godfrey Higgins says 'The symbolical type of the sun, the redeemer, or of the first Sign in which the sun had his exaltation and completed his victory over the powers of darkness, has been carefully preserved in the religion of the Christians, so that to name Christ or the Lamb is the same thing as to name the Redeemer .... The mysteries of the Lamb are mysteries of the same nature as those of the Mythraitic Bull, to which they succeeded by the effect of the precession of the equinoxes, which substituted the slain Lamb for the slain Bull. The Christian mysteries of the lamb are proved to be taken from the mysteries of Mithra, of the Persians, by the circumstance that the Persians alone have the lamb for the symbol of the equinoctial sign: the other nations have the full grown Ram.'

M. Dupuis observes that 'the lamb was a symbol or mark of intiation into the Christian mysteries, a sort of proof of admission into the societies of the initiated of the lamb, like the private sign of the freemasons'. The Templars, who were the keepers of the Holy Grail, held this 'sign' in great reverence, for the celestial vault was their Templum.

It is remarkable, with the strong zodiacal tradition running through Rosicrucian, Templar, and Masonic records, that students of the Arthurian Cycle should never, so far as I know, connect it with the Round Table. My discovery of the actual prehistoric zodiac — on which the legends are founded — laid out upon the Holy Land of Glastonbury, definitely revealed this connection.

According to Hargrave Jennings in *The Rosicrucians, their Rites and Mysteries,* the Round Table of the Knights of King Arthur is typical of the San Greal, in imitation of the Holy Supper, which was partaken of at a Round Table, with the Twelve Disciples and the Round Table instituted by Joseph in imitation of the Holy Supper was called 'Graal' in the Romance of Merlin. Jennings says also, 'The Round Table of King Arthur is a Grand Mythological Synthesis. It is a whole Mythology in itself. It is perennial. It is Christian. By tradition it devolves from the very earliest period. It is the English "Palladium".' He shows

an excellent illustration of the Round Table preserved in
the Court-House of the Castle of Winchester, which was
repainted in the time of Henry VIII, it has twelve light and
twelve dark divisions radiating from the central rose,[3] and
he calls it 'The Round Table of King Arthur, Sangreal or
Holy Grail'. Further, speaking of the Rose window in Laon
Cathedral, Jennings affirms 'The twelve pillars or
"radii" are the signs of the Zodiac, and are issuant out of
the glorified centre, or opening "rose", — the sun or
"beginning all things", which is crucified in the heavens
at the vernal Equinox.'

The fact that Freemasons are specifically charged to
study geometry and astronomy is proof in itself that
Masonry has the same scientific foundation as that upon
which the Arthurian traditions stand. But *The High
History of the Holy Grail* declares King Arthur saw five
changes in the Grail 'the last where-of was the change
into a Chalice'.

Hargrave Jennings says the Zodiac 'yet remains the key
to all the mythologies and all religions', and again, 'It is
no inconsistent thing to say that, in the Rosicrucian sense,
every stone, flower, and tree has its horoscope, and that
they are produced and flourish in the mechanical resources
of the mysterious necessities of astrology.'

The doctrine of the Macrocosm and the Microcosm in all
ages has been set forth under a variety of symbolic
statements, for example:

Heaven above, heaven below;
Stars above, Stars below;
All that is over, under shall show.
Happy thou who the riddle readest.[4]

Tabula Smaragdina

Apply the above to the heavens laid out on earth in
Somerset and at once we realize what a dynamic reality
this Grail countryside must have been to the astrologers
who transformed it.

It is abundantly evident, since the discovery of this
actual 'garden of the god', that the Arthurian legends
were originally based on an agricultural cult as well as
that of the sun and stars; possibly this is the reason why
'the Quest' has always proved so bewildering, not only to

the knights who sought the Grail, but also to scholars, such as John Rhys who admits 'We have here ventured to treat Arthur as a Culture Hero; it is quite possible that this is mythologically wrong, and that he should in fact rather be treated, let us say, as a Keltic Zeus.'

James Breasted said 'Like the Egyptians, the earliest Babylonians had beheld their gods in the forces of nature, and their earliest divinities were nature gods. In a remarkable hymn which must have been employed in the worship of Sin, the Moon-god, in his temple at Ur, we find the priestly author clearly disclosing the background of nature in which he involuntarily beheld the Moon-god functioning':

When thy word resoundeth in heaven, the gods of the upper world throw themselves down on their faces;
When thy word resoundeth on earth, the gods of the lower world kiss the ground, etc.

But to pedestrians like Mr. Mais, whilst 'Walking in Somerset,' such gods are still 'invisible'. He would find 'greater pleasure in the glorious avenue of beeches through which I could see Glastonbury Tor neatly framed over the fields and woodlands ... and yet another avenue, the loveliest of all, a wide cedar avenue going off at right angles on both sides of the road, with a well-marked green track down the middle'. The first skirts the ridge along the neck of Taurus, and the second leads to Leo's ear, and this is what he says of the road leading from the tip of the tail of Aries to the front leg: 'At Piper's Road House, I crossed the Taunton-Glastonbury road and climbed a lovely open down. This was Walton Hill and soon I was on the smooth, open upland of Ivythorn Hill, a fine National Trust property, with a glorious view of all the marshes of Somerton Moor. Except for a farm at the foot of the hill, which fell steeply on my right, I could see no house in all the marshes. It was just one vast estuary with the tide a long time out.'

And so it was on these Polden Hills where lie the Ram, the Bull and the Lion, that the *Guide to Glastonbury's Temple of the Stars* was written; there in the high 'Tower' above Chilton Polden, where 'the White Lady of Sedge Moor' beats up against its grey stone walls, the discovery of the Somerset Zodiac was made.

'The land of the dead where the shadowy phantoms of the heroes of old time sat croned, each upon his throne.'

The Welsh bard Taleisin wrote a poem entitled, *A View of the Bardic Sanctuary*, which unmistakably describes the Round Table of the Zodiac in Somerset and consequently of high archaeological value, I quote:

A holy sanctuary there is, on the wide lake; a city not protected with walls; the sea surrounds it. Demandest thou, O Britain, to what this can be meetly applied! Before the lake of the son of Erbin, let thy ox be stationed. The sacred ox of the patriarch is stationed before the lake, ready to draw the shrine to land out of the watery repository. It is the lake of the vessel of the lofty chiefs. The eagle, or symbol of the sun, was placed aloft in the sky, that is, in the open aethereal temple, which is often so called. There was the representation of the path of Apollo — an image of the ecliptic, in which the pomp was conducted, preceded by the waving eagle. And this was done in the presence of the great sovereign, or the sun himself.[1]

The same source tells us, 'The prison of Gowair is here called Caer Sidi, the circle of the zodiac, in which their luminous emblems, the sun, moon and planets, revolve, the sanctuary of the British Ceries, which represented both the ark and the zodiac.'

Edward Davies did not know of the Temple of the Stars in the neighbourhood of Glastonbury, but it is quite apparent that the Welsh Bards, especially Taliesin, had detailed records of it. Before the sea walls were built the sea used to come up to the effigy ship of the giant Orion, and there stationed beside this 'vessel' lies the sacred ox, Taurus.

'The great sovereign' is aptly described by Lewis Spence in his *Mystery of Britain* as follows, 'If we turn now to the higher philosophy of British mysticism as expressed in Barddas, we find Supreme Power described as inconceivable and incomprehensible. The allusion seems to be to Hu who is further identified with the Heus of the Gauls, alluded to as the Supreme proprietor of the Isle of

Britain in Welsh myth, and who appears to have been
symbolized by the ox, much as the Apis bull represented
Osiris. That Heus was also represented in ox form is
practically certain, and a number of Keltic place-names
suggest that they were sites of a bull cult.'

'The eagle' or Phoenix, the symbol of the Sun, set high
on Glastonbury Tor, has already been described.

As regards 'the vessel of the lofty chief', Dudley Wright
in his *Druidism* says, 'In common with most nations the
Druids had their Deluge traditions, but represented the
event as occurring in a lake called Llyn Llion, the waters
of which burst forth and overwhelmed the face of the
whole world. One vessel only escaped the catastrophe, and
in this were a man and woman and certain of the animal
species. By these Britain was re-peopled with human
beings and animals. The name given to the man thus
miraculously preserved was Hu, the Mighty. He is
frequently represented as the diluvial god, and as such is
generally attended by a spotted cow. The woman was
"the goddess of the various seeds".'

Here we have mentioned the effigy goddess Virgo, who
flings her great bunch of 'various seeds' across the whole
width of the 'path of Apollo'; and again the Mighty Hu
with his ark, and spotted star cow, (Gemini and Taurus),
and Leo's 'lion lake' caused by the River Cary which
outlines the effigy lion and, bursting its banks every year,
floods the whole of King Sedge Moor like a vast lake.

I have often seen Sedge Moor completely submerged, a
few isolated farm houses marooned and dependent on
boats for weeks in winter. These local boats have a
dangerous time in the swirling waters, which sweep them
into the branches of trees.

As for this 'spotted cow', or 'sacred ox', or Bull, though
on the Somerset zodiac and also on star maps, only its
head and right fore leg are represented. Nevertheless, it is
in one respect the most important of all the 'signs',
because it led the year when this earthly or 'mundane
circle' was conceived. Taurus and Argo are connected with
the moon; possibly that is the reason why it lays its hoof
on the top of the main mast of the Giant Twin's ship, the
'vessel' mentioned above.[2]

Thus only by legend and tradition preserved in Barddas, the Arthurian Cycle, Keltic folklore and the like, can we hope to recover the facts concerning the prehistoric Temple of our ancestors that has been so laboriously reconstructed from standard maps, air photographs of the earthwork effigies, and star charts. But it is remarkable, with so many different indications pointing to the 'nether sky,' as Homer calls the heaven of the heroes of Troy, that the Somerset zodiac should not have been found long ago in what he names the lonely northern land of the 'nation of Cimmeria', for the Cymri living in Wales came from the neighbourhood of Troy. In Homer's Odyssey we read that Ulysses arrived at this 'nether sky':

The ship we moor on these obscure abodes;
Disbark the sheep, an offering to the gods;
And, hellward bending, o'er the beach descry
The doleful passage to the infernal sky.

The British Edda, found in Iceland, also calls the home of the Giants hell.

A nether and an infernal sky could mean only the star constellations laid out on earth like those near Glastonbury, which are now divided from Wales by the Severn river, for Ulysses and his companions were alive and made no actual descent into hell but landed on the sea beach and at once encountered beings:

More fierce than giants, more than giants strong;
The earth o'erburden'd groaned beneath their weight,
None but Orion e'er surpassed their height, . . .
His shafts Apollo aim'd; at once they sound,
And stretch the giant monsters o'er the ground.

Translated by Pope. Book XI.

Brutus of Troy, when he came to Britain, was told that it had been inhabited by giants, doubtless those described by Homer, 'Stern Minos, high on a throne, tremendous to behold', and 'Hercules, a towering spectre of gigantic mould', for of such were these 'giant monsters o'er the ground' in Somerset.

Plutarch tells us that the principal object of adoration among the Cimbri, in the time of Marius, was a brazen bull by which they were accustomed to swear on solemn occasions; and that to the west of Britain a festival was held at the end of every thirty years which was connected with Taurus. To show how a belief will persist for four or five thousand years, the Highlanders of Scotland still believe that in the twilight on New Year's Eve the figure of a gigantic bull, called the 'Candlemas Bull', is to be seen crossing the heavens.

In like manner of perpetuity the Virgin Mary is seen seated upon the crescent moon or with the moon and stars in her hair as Queen of Heaven; thousands of agriculturists still regulate their sowing of seeds by the waxing or waning of the moon. Christ seated in the sun surrounded by rays, with the earth and moon at His feet, is equally familiar in symbolic art, and on the arms of His cross are shown the star constellation creatures, called rather humorously the Evangelistic symbols — the Bull, the Lion, the Man, and the Eagle — which respectively marked the vernal equinox, summer solstice, autumnal equinox and winter solstice from about 4000 to 2000 B.C. and will outlast all other religious symbols, for the sun will continue to revolve against the background of the fixed stars. What more profound and beautiful symbology could be found anywhere else!

Plutarch seems to have been very interested in this Taurus, for to quote him again, in his 36th Question he asks:'Why do the women of Elis summon Dionysos in their hymns to be present with them with his bull-foot?' and gives their ritual hymn thus:

In Spring-time, O Dionysos, to thy holy temple come;
Rushing with thy bull-foot come, noble Bull, Noble Bull.

'Is it,' he suggests, 'that some entitle the god as 'Born of a Bull' and as a 'Bull' himself? Or is it that many hold the god is the beginning of sowing and ploughing? (See *Ancient Art and Ritual* by Jane Harrison.)

SIGNS AND SECRETS 5: Gemini

It was once believed that the soul of Osiris rested in the constellation Orion; the stars of Orion fall upon the Somerset effigy of the Giant sun-god who sits in the moon boat Argo. The Giant and his boat represent together the sun and moon, Gemini the twins, and suggest Osiris or Horus sitting in 'the Boat of Millions of Years' which stood still when the child Horus was stung by Scorpio. When this happened, Thoth descended from it; he had with him the Word which all heaven and earth and hell must obey; having uttered it, a portion of the 'fluid of life' from Ra passed into Horus and brought him to life.[1]

So it is the Word we have reason to look for in this 'sign.' Let us now collect what evidence we can.

In Somerset the effigy Giant child, like Horus, emblem of the perpetual rebirth of nature, is designed as contrast to the old bearded god on the other side of the circle of zodiacal effigies, who, in the constellation of the Archer, has shot his arrow, or ray, 'the fluid of life' into this child in the west.

The learned Eratosthenes, speaking of the Sun-god's famous arrow, says 'he hid it amongst the Hyperboreans, where there is his winged temple.'

The two masts of the effigy moon boat, when projected, converge upon the zenith of this winged temple of the stars, thus forming a triangle (the geometrical ground work of the circular lay out) and the main mast thus passes through the first magnitude stars, Aldebaran and Capella in Auriga. Capella was regarded as the patron star of Babylon because to the Assyrians it was the leader of the year, for in ancient times the commencement of the year was fixed by the position of Capella in relation to the moon at the spring equinox when its horns turned upwards, whilst Aldebaran marked the equinox of about 2700 B.C. The constellation Gemini used to be represented by the figure of two stars over a ship, and in the story of the Argonauts it was this favourable sign to seamen that saved the ship Argo.

The ancient Boundary Stones of Babylon show the sun, star and moon together: the crescent moon lies on its back. I well remember the moon in that position out in the Arabian desert when we were racing through the night from Bagdad to Palmyra: so clear is the air in the desert that the moon seemed to hang almost within reach as it rose and passed over the sky and then lay down to sleep, horns pointing upwards, apparently quite close to us. It thus suggested the cup of the Grail. When the thirteen moon months were calculated to make up a year, the moon was in that position and looked like a ship that sailed round the year.

Place names on an old site are historically illuminating; for instance the Parrett River of Somerset, which outlines the 'great dog' of this 'Kingdom of Logres', is perhaps the oldest name in the British Isles. It was left by the Sumerian settlers, Somerset being 'The Seat of the Sumers' or Cymry. So, close to the effigy that portrays the constellation Gemini we find the ancient names for the Sun gods, Lug and Hu, in Lugshorn and Huish, and in Dundon Hayes Lane which outlines this god of Wisdom's body.

Lysons says in *Our British Ancestors*: 'Hue — the manifestor, instructor, the teacher; Chaldee Hoa — to shew, to declare.' The presiding deity of the abyss or the great deep in the Babylonian mythology, his important titles refer to the source of all knowledge and science. 'And now the lofty leader Huan is about to ascend — the sovereign most glorious — the Lord of the British Isles.' The 'Hu gadan' of the British poems, 'the deified patriarch', corresponding with Noah. The worship of Noah was, at first in Chaldea and later in Egypt, strangely united with the worship of the sun. Osiris the Egyptian sun-god was a deification of Noah, and he entered into the Ark, which was symbolized by the crescent moon.

That explains how our Giant sun effigy happens to be the twin of the moon. He is sitting in the moon boat Argo, which was said to be the first ship ever built. He holds the stars of Gemini that lie on the ecliptic in his upraised right hand. The ancient Druids had ceremonies at every change of the moon, more especially at the time of the new moon.

The custom of bowing to the new moon is still practised in some country places in England where its origin has long been forgotten.

Lysons makes a very important statement in regard to this god Hue, or Hoa 'the teacher of man-kind, the Lord of understanding'. He says: 'One of his emblems is the wedge, or arrow-head, the essential element in the cuneiform writing, which seems to assign to him the invention, or at least patronage, of the Chaldean alphabet; Berosus represents him as one of the primeval gods', which is now proved.

Here we have that 'Greatest Secret of the whole wide world' referred to in the Prologue to the Grand Saint Graal, for a word takes shape in writing and it was this 'Giant that first made a letter'.

The oldest literature of Britain records that the 'Son of the Three Shouts' beheld the original language, which began with the Name of God, 'When God pronounced His Name, with the Word sprang the Light and Life.'

The science preserved by the wise men of the nation of the Cymry tells how 'the Giant (Hu) beheld three pillars of light, (the arrows of the sun) on which were inscribed all the sciences that ever were. It was the Giant that first made a letter which was the form of God's Name.' That Giant's letter resembles the 'arrow-head' or 'broad-arrow' which represents the Cymric name of God, consequently this is the most valuable tradition and the oldest of the origin of writing, still preserved, for it is 'the essential element in cuneiform writing'.

The Encyclopaedia says that the cuneiform script was invented by the Sumerians and that the literary idiom of the Babylonian wise men was the non-Semitic Sumerian, their writing cuneiform.

As to those 'wise men', in Daniel the term 'Chaldeans' is very commonly employed with the meaning 'astrologers, astronomers', which sense also appears in the classical authors, notably in Herodotus, Strabo and Diodorus. In Daniel i. 4, by the expression 'tongue of the Chaldeans', the writer evidently meant the language in which the celebrated Babylonian works on astrology and divination were composed.

Not only the 'broad arrow', or name of God, suggested by the slanting masts of the ship, but also the bell, called in the High History 'clappers', which is engraved under the Bull's neck, are 'the most valid and efficacious symbols' carried by 'the Ship of the Secret Faith' to 'the end of a certain time', 'the secret of the Grail itself'.

Lewis Spence points out that the Mystic Letters of the name of God were the foundation of the secret tradition of Britain, the 'insula sacra' of the West.

Liver Moor Drove Outlines Poop of Ship

The Giant Huan's 'letter' being cuneiform again suggests that the makers of the Somerset zodiac were of Sumerian origin; that being so it is not surprising to find the place name Liver Moor just below the Giant's knee. The Chaldeans divined by means of a liver to interpret the oracles of the gods and the Babylonians believed that the seat of all passions was not the heart but the liver; in the Book of Ezekiel xxi, 2, we read that the King of Babylon 'looked in the liver'; that was in the sixth century B.C.

Liver divining was practiced in Nineveh a century earlier, which is proved by the clay model of a liver, inscribed with omens, now in the British Museum. Other excavations have brought to light a considerable number of clay models of an animal's liver inscribed in cuneiform with remarks in the Babylonian and Hittite languages; whilst an Etruscan liver, cast in bronze, and now at Piacenza, resembles the foetus as does our Giant.

Sargon of Agade and Naram-Sin, who lived between 2637 and 2582 B.C., made use of omens derived from the livers of sheep, as illustrated by Wallis Budge in *Amulets and Superstitions*.

A place name that tells another story is Redlands, for this Giant Twin and the surrounding countryside is composed of red marl; consequently we find on the map not only Redlands in front and behind him, but Red Lake outlines the boat in which he sits. This is significant, because the ancients connected red earth with life, as on the Island of Teneriffe which is thought by some to be the last peak of Atlantis; thousands of mummies were found in the red strata of the caves; these I have visited, and picked up bones stained red from contact with the red rock.

The High History of the Holy Grail places the chief tournaments in which King Arthur and his knights contested at Red laund; before the war one could see circles on the Fair Field left by the modern fair that was held, very likely, on the same ground on which the tilting contests took place, for it is the only suitable field between the swamps of the sea-moors and the steep red hills.

Given these clues, a peculiar place name, Emblett Lane, which outlines the stomach of the Giant, is worth study, because this Orion sits between the two masts of his ship, on the base line of the triangle, which gives the exact measurement of the thirteenth moon month of the layout of the calendar. The name suggests that this was the month that was 'intercalated' to fill in the irregularities of a year, that secret thirteenth moon month of the Templars, who were the keepers of the Grail.

Ember means a season of fasting and humiliation or it may mean, directly from Anglo Saxon, 'the circle or course of the year' from emb, round. In the Church of England Calendar it is used in ember-days, ember-tide, ember-week, and ember-fast. From the Greek root comes 'embolism' meaning 'intercalation or the insertion of days or months in an account of time to produce regularity'.

This being the case, we have the explanation of why Argo Navis, the star constellation below the giant Orion, is always depicted on star maps as only half a ship with no prow! Here on the Round Table of King Arthur's zodiac is a measurement recorded between its two masts intended to be remembered for all time, the measurement of that sidereal thirteen moon month — 27 degrees 41 minutes 32 seconds of the 360 degrees of this Temple's circumference.

This is an instance why ancient signs and symbols should not be tampered with, for every picture originally set in the heavens was intended to speak for itself. The Somerset effigy ship gives us the meaning so long sought of the prowless Argo Navis.

Books on the constellation figures say that this is the celebrated ship of the Argonauts, of which Homer sang ten centuries before Christ. Sir Isaac Newton puts the expedition of the Argonauts shortly after the death of Solomon (about 975 B.C.), while Dr. Blair's chronology puts it at 1236 B.C., but according to records of solar eclipses the exact date of the return of Ulysses was April 16th, 1178 B.C., for Homer tells in the Odyssey that 'The sun has perished out of heaven' and the eclipse was total around Ithaca, where Ulysses lived, on that date. Some people think that the story had its origin in name as well as in fact from the Ark of Noah.

Considering the tradition in English history that King Brutus came of Trojan stock, the Argonaut story might well apply here, but the Giant child who is seated in the Ark was certainly conceived over a thousand years earlier and may have had his boat reconstructed by the Argonauts, as it is the only effigy in the whole lay-out that is entirely delineated by straight lines.

As for the legends that King Solomon built the ship of the Graal; Solomon, in the Arthurian Romances, must be read Sol the Sun, for its masts slope like rays from the sun at the zenith, pointing to that mythical bird of the Winged Temple, which I am tempted to call the Ember Goose, whose breast and belly are silver like the moon and whose wings and tail feathers are black as the night. Of Hansa the goose, Madame Blavatsky says: 'the symbol of Hansa the goose is an important symbol, representing for instance, Divine Wisdom, Wisdom in darkness beyond the reach of men.... Hansa is the symbol of that male or temporary deity, as he, the emanation of the primordial Ray, is made to serve as a Vahan or vehicle for that divine Ray, which otherwise could not manifest itself in the Universe, being, antiphrastically, itself an emanation of "Darkness".... As to the strange symbol chosen it is equally suggestive; the true mystic significance being the idea of a universal matrix, figured by the primordial waters of the "deep", or the opening for the reception, and subsequently for the issue, of that one ray (the Logos), which contains in itself the other seven procreative rays or powers'. (*The Secret Doctrine*, p.80).

'A physical basis is necessary to focus a Ray of the Universal Mind and link them together, thus the Ray is the animating principle electrifying every atom into life, Spirit-matter, Life, the "Spirit of the Universe" or the second Logos.'

Therefore, in Arthurian Romance Merlin told Uther, 'and this is what yon star doth betoken. The ray doth portend that a son shall be born unto thee that shall be of surpassing mighty dominion'. That son was King Arthur of Britain. 'There appeared a star of marvellous brightness and bigness, stretching forth one ray whereon was a ball of fire spreading forth in the likeness of a dragon, and from the mouth of the dragon issued forth two rays, whereof the one was of such length as that it did seem to reach beyond the region of Gaul and the other, verging toward the Irish sea, did end in seven lesser rays.'

Compare the Navajo Creation Myth with the foregoing.[2] 'A great Star appeared over the Mountain. The Star was the Fire god, he sent a Light-ray down to the mountain. The Talking god then appeared dressed in a rainbow and spake four times to the people who told him to "go and see why there was a light on the mountain" and he saw the Light-ray connecting the mountain and the sky and he heard all sorts of birds singing. When he went up to the mountain he found a very fine new-born baby, the child of the Earth Spirit and Sky Spirit'. Here we have our effigy Giant child again, and the ray.

The Welsh Barddas gives us the explanation of this 'secret of the whole wide world'. 'The letters of the Holy Name are called the three columns of truth, because there can be no knowledge of truth but from the light thrown upon it: and the three columns of the sciences because there can be no sciences, but from the light and truth', and again, 'Having obtained Earth under him coinstantaneously with the Light, he drew the form of the voice and light on the Earth.'

The Writing on the Grail
In The Garden of Paradise

As the Templars were the traditional keepers of the Holy Grail, of which King Arthur's Round Table of the Stars was the pattern, let us try to read between the lines of a Templar who wrote soon after A.D. 1100 and thus find the secret of Wolfram von Eschenbach's Parzival, which he calls 'a parable so fleeting too swift for the dull shall be'.

Nevertheless, to those who know the meaning of the writing 'in the palm of mine hand', he reveals his secret immediately, as a Freemason might in 'the mystery of a close grasp he sure doth know'; the 'writing on the Grail' was a more closely guarded secret than even the starry bowl, that received its inspiration from on high.

Most people are inclined to treat the Arthurian 'Romances' purely as fairy tales, and even A.E. Waite, though realizing some profound significance in them, shows his ignorance by making fun of Wolfram von Eschenbach's Parzival, which however is one of the most knowledgeable versions, and might well have been 'written in a pagan tongue'! Mr. Waite says (*The Holy Grail*, page 274); 'Behind Kyot there was pictured Flegitanis, descended from the wise Solomon and one who was renowned for his knowledge, especially concerning the stars, he being an astronomer above all things. It came about therefore that beeind Flegitanis were all the starry heavens and that by his ability to read therein he became qualified to affirm the existence of a "prodigy" called the Grail ... and Kyot, with all his celestial signs revolving in heaven above him. ... He could have done much better in one respect, unless indeed he intended to betray his own invention: he need not have made Flegitanis a pagan who worshipped a calf; he need not have put him far back into pre-Christian days.'

But the 'celestial signs' are the very texture of the whole fabric. Of course Flegitanis was 'a pagan who worshipped a calf' and the other celestial signs: it was obviously 'by his ability to read therein' he became qualified to afirm the existence of the so-called Grail.

Learned scholars are not infallible, and it is quite likely that Kyot did indeed 'discover a pre-Christian Arabic text lying neglected at Toledo'.

The story commences when 'at Bagdad did reign a monarch so strong and powerful, that homage he well might claim from two-thirds or more of earth's kingdoms'. One's mind at once reverts to those Sumerian rules from whom the Somerset Zodiac derives.

Thus we see that Wolfram von Eschenbach was using a definitely authentic source for his Grail Romance, despite

the slur cast upon his Toledo manuscript; and it is also
likely to be true that the knight who wounded the King of
the Grail came from the River Tigris, as he states, because
the red wound on the thigh of the effigy Orion (King
Anfortas) was made by a 'heathen' whose purpose in
wounding the king was that 'he should win the Grail and
should hold it', for it was 'the fame of the Grail drew him
thither'. This wound seems to hold the secret of the keeper
of the Grail's kingdom, for the text says, 'yet King shall he
be no longer tho' healing and bliss he know;' also the
fateful question that Parzival had to ask hinges upon this
particular wound.

As a matter of fact, it is upon the wound that the central
Ray of the three fold Word falls, the wound corresponding
with the famous star Rigel, in the constellation Orion. [3]
Rigel is one of the most luminous stars in all the heavens
and sparkles like a white diamond, recalling the lines,
'upon the wound they lay it (the spear) and the frost from
his flesh so cold it drawest, and lo! as crystals of glass to
the spear doth hold, and as ice to the iron it clingeth, and
none looseth it from the blade'.

Consequently there can be little doubt that the Giant
Orion is the effigy in question, for the centre of the boat
from which King Anfortas used to fish, the ship of the
Grail[4] also used by Parzival, lies exactly below Rigel. So
with the evidence of this 'Mysterious Ship, destined to sail
the seas for centuries', whose masts converge on the sun;
and the red wound on which hung 'the Enchantments of
Britain'; and the Tamuz month on the calendar; and the
world wide legends about the wounding of other resurrection gods, Adonis, Osiris, Tamuz, Mithra and the rest; and
also that the Sword which could 'enforce an entrance into
the Earthly Paradise,' and was a Hallow of the Grail, was
kept here where Orion naturally kept his world famous
sword; we conclude this is the most likely place in which to
find 'the writing on the Grail'.

The ceremonies attending the resurrection gods imply
the alternate return of summer and winter; the festivals
always began with mournful lamentations, finishing with
a revival of joy as they returned to life. We find the same
lamentation characterizing the Grail history, and on

Parzival's visit to Anfortas 'thro' the lofty palace was weeping and wailing sore, the folk of thirty kingdoms could scarce have bemoaned them more'.

Now if we turn to the last 'book' of Wolfram von Eschenbach's Parzival, we see that the Temlars have been keeping the king Anfortas alive with the sight of the Holy Grail, 'from the might of Its mystic virtue fresh life must ever draw', for its essential quality is 'fresh life' and 'the word' had been seen 'writ on the Grail' that should cure him by the aid of Parzival.

So the future Grail-keeper, Parzival, arrives at the castle with his 'black and white' brother; and 'the twain did Anfortas welcome with gladness, and yet with grief, and spake, "O'er long have I waited tho' I win from thine hand relief."' In answer to the wounded king's query, 'Now say where the Grail itlieth?', Parzival 'three times on his knee he bowed him in the Name of the Trinity' and asked 'what aileth thee here, mine uncle?'

That last fateful question is never answered, but the king's question 'now say where the Grail it lieth' is answered by Parzival's gesture of genuflexion 'in the Name of the Trinity', 'here', in front of the wound, and at once Anfortas is healed and his face shone with radiant beauty; no doubt illumined by the three-fold rays of the holy Name. Also when Parzival tells the news of the healing, a hermit replies, 'God is Man, and the Word of His Father; God is Father at once and Son, and I wot thro' His Spirit's working, may succour and aid be won!'

The Welsh Bards have retained this Word which was not allowed to be uttered, (hence Parzival's gesture), from the earliest times of Sumerian colonization; and 'when swearing in the Name of God, a Bard stood within the form or figure of the Divine Name, which was, as it were imperceptibly drawn on the Gorsedd'. That is to say, at the time the sun rises and on equinoctial and solstitial days, casts its rays over the 'station stones', 'the rays should traverse them in the direction of the stone of the covenant, in the centre of the circle', as for example on a sun-dial, or like a broad-arrow.

Wolfram von Eschenbach tells us it was written upon the Grail that no one should ask what country, or name, or race its priests came from, the reason being that just as the zodiacal creatures were pre-Christian, so the writing was of the same age, for we have already been told that the Holy Grail existed at the time the monarch of Bagdad ruled over 'two-thirds or more of the earth's kingdoms'.

'Twas a heathen, Flagetanis, who had won for his wisdom fame...

And he was the first of earth's children the lore of the Grail to tell.

By his father's side a heathen, a calf he for God did hold,[5]

And the heathen, Flagetanis, could read in the heavens high

How the stars roll on their courses, how they circle the silent sky

And the time when their wandering endeth — and the life and the lot of men

He read in the stars, and strange secrets he saw, and he spake again

Low, with bated breath and fearful, of the thing that is called the Grail

In a cluster of stars was it written, the Name, nor their lore shall fail....[6]

And the sons of baptized men hold It, and guard It with humble heart,

And the best of mankind shall those knights be who have in such service part.[7]

The Hidden Name

This 'Word' for which so many have searched has been known as 'the Lost Word', 'the Word of Power', 'the Secret Name of God'. A quaint Jewish legend of the Middle Ages says the 'Hidden Name' was secretly inscribed in the innermost recesses of the Temple; but that, even if discovered, which was most unlikely, it could not be retained because guarding it was a sculptured lion which gave such a supernatural roar as the intruder was quitting the spot all memory of the 'Hidden Name' was driven from his mind. Jesus, however, says the legend, knew this and evaded the lion. He transcribed the Name and, cutting open his thigh,[8] hid the writing in the incision, which by

magic art, he at once closed up; then, after leaving the
Temple, he took the writing out and so retained the
knowledge of the Name.

To quote from the *Secret Doctrine*, 'If one turns to the
ancient literature of the Semitic religions, to the Chaldean
Scriptures, the elder sister and instructress, if not the
fountain-head of the Mosaic Bible, the basis and starting-
point of Christianity, what do the scholars find? To
perpetuate the memory of the ancient religions of Babylon;
to record the vast cycle of astronomical observations of the
Chaldean Magi; to justify the traditions of their splendid
and eminently occult literature what now remains? Only a
few fragments.'

But so many 'fragments' have been found since that
was written we can now explain literally what this strange
Semitic legend means by reference to the Temple of the
Stars in Somerset where that 'sculptured' or effigy Lion
(Leo) guards the 'Hidden Name'. For, let us repeat, 'the
science' preserved by the wise men of the nation of the
Cymry tells how 'the Giant beheld three pillars of light, on
which were inscribed all the sciences that ever were'; the
sciences were taught therefrom, but this 'Name of God
was kept secret'. 'It was the Giant that first made a letter,
which was the form of God's Name.'

Now the effigy Giant towards whom the Lion is looking
is the effigy of Orion, and this is where we find the three-
rayed name for God. We further read, 'the symbol of God's
Name from the beginning; in three columns; and in the
Rays of Light the vocalization — for one were the hearing
and the seeing'. These rays penetrate Mother Earth and
she in turn brings forth her harvest of eternal festival;
consequently it is interesting to note that the same symbol,
the Broad Arrow — pregnant with archaic religious
significance — is still used as the Royal mark on British
Government Stores of every description.

There is a Masonic document, written as long ago as
1730, which calls itself 'The Grand Secret or the Form of
giving the Masonic Word'; this was reprinted in *The
Speculative Mason* of July, 1937. Under the title 'Giants',
is explained the position of the central line, or the Secret
Doctrine's 'Ray, dropped into the great Cosmic depths'. I

find if this line is projected on the map of the Temple it
cuts through the Giant Orion's thigh! There are many
other wounded thigh legends. For instance, Dionysos was
called 'He of the double door' because he was born 'once of
his mother like all men, once of his father's thigh like no
man'; his second birth thus implies another kind of birth,
i.e. the initiation rite of 'Bringing to Light', hence the Ray
of the sun here on the folded leg of the Giant Orion in
order that he could 'walk' as in the Egyptian myth; or
become like Dionysos 'the Divine Leaper, Dancer and
lifegiver'[9]. To prove the applicability of these legends to
this particular calendrical effigy, every year when the
minehead 'phantom ship' is paraded — not many miles
from this Dundon hill — the man with the boat continual-
ly crouches down and leaps up singing:

Awake, St. George, our English knight Oh!
For summer is a come and winter is a go,
And every day God gives us his grace,
By day and night Oh!

and in this prehistoric zodiac the Giant lies directly under
the convergence of the two masts or Pillars of his Ship
upon the central enclosure of the sun. The space between
them at their base gives us the exact measurement of the
thirteenth division of the Temple circumference. Jesus was
the 13th amongst his twelve disciples; and the Kabalistic
saying is, 'in the thirteenth hour, It (the Deity) shall
restore all'.

On the exquisitely sculptured celestial globe, that the
Giant Orion or Atlas supports with his shoulders, in the
National Museum at Naples, this mark of three converging lines born by the Sun's Ship is the most
conspicuous object, directly above the Giant's forehead. It
is obviously meant as a symbol, as if projected from his
mind, of the Trinity or astronomical triad, the 'Divine
Word', the Primeval Light from which countless lights
were lit.

That pre-Christian sculpture thus confirms the Holy
Grail legends of 'the building of a Ship of the Secret Faith,
that at the end of a certain time it might carry into the far
distance the most valid and efficacious symbol', 'the
Mysterious Ship of Solomon which haunts the sea in the

Grand Saint Grail containing the secret of the Grail itself'.
The actual star constellation effigies could never have
been given their triangular divisions to fit the dome of the
sky without three Rays from the centre, which, like the
rays of the sun that swing round and round it every day,
draw the endless Circle of Time. They are the celestial
Compasses, the Pillars of the Law, and the Symbol of
God's Name from the beginning.

When the Hermit of the Grand Saint Grail is first
received into that state of vision, what he is promised is
a revelation of the Greatest Secret of the whole wide
world, so small indeed that it can lie in the hollow of the
Hermit's hand. This notwithstanding, it is the greatest
marvel that man can ever receive, but which to
pronounce aloud would convulse the elemental world.
Look in the hollow of your own hand and you will see the
three converging Rays of the Hidden Name!

The subject is endless, but four 'fragments' from The
Chaldean Oracles must suffice:

In every cosmos there shineth a Triad, of which a
Monad is source.

The Centre, from which all rays to the periphery are equal.

All things are served in the Gulps of the Triad.

The Mind of the Father, vehicled in rare Drawers-
of-Straight-lines, lashes inflexibly in furrows of
implacable Fire.

The Vocal God of Light

A remarkable legend, in the life of St. Patrick, a Keltic
saint who settled in Glastonbury organizing the solitary
hermits there, records how he, having crossed the water,
saw 'an idol, the Head or Chief of the Mound, covered with
gold and silver, and twelve other idols about it, covered
with brass'. This idol was seen from the water 'to bow its
head Westwards, for its face was from the South' (which
exactly describes the position of the head of the Dundon
Hill Giant looking towards the Severn Sea).

Though St. Patrick did not touch the idol yet the mark of
Jesus' crozier abides on its left side still, we are told, and
'the twelve other images can be seen to this day half
engulfed in the earth'.

This 'Bent one of the Mound' can be none other than

Orion in the Somerset Circle of the Zodiac, and 'Jesus'
crozier' the mystic Ray. The legend proves that up to the
seventh century A.D. when the saint's life was written, the
details of its posture, as well as its gold for the sun and
silver for the moon, was still fresh in memory.

As it was one of the sidereal Time gods, perhaps random
extracts from the Book of Dyzan may suggest its conception, and throw light on the whole question of the Holy
Grail from this entirely new angle of 'Time'.

Time was not, for it lay asleep in the infinite bosom of
duration.

Where were the Builders, the Luminous Sons?

The hour had not yet struck: the Ray had not yet flashed
into the Germ.

Her heart had not yet opened for the one Ray to enter,
thence to fall, as three into four, into the lap of Maya.

Darkness radiates Light and Light drops one solitary
Ray into the Mother-deep.

From the effulgence of Light — the Ray of the ever-
darkness — sprung in space the re-awakened energies.

From the Divine Man emanated the forms, the sparks,
the sacred animals, and the messengers of the sacred
Fathers within the Holy Four.

This was the army of the Voice. These 'sparks' are
called spheres, triangles, cubes, lines and modellers.

The one Ray multiplies the small rays. Life precedes
form, and life survives the last atom of form. Through
the countless

rays proceeds the life Ray, the One, like a thread
through many jewels.

(See Seven Stanzas.)

Dr. Angus in his work on *The Mystery Religions and
Christianity* expresses this larger cosmic sense thus:
'Never was there an age which heard so distinctly and
responded so willingly to the call of the Cosmos to its
inhabitants. The unity of all Life, the mysterious harmony
of the least and nearest with the greatest and most remote,
the conviction that the Life of the Universe pulsated in all
its parts, were as familiar to that ancient Cosmic Con-
sciousness as to modern biology and psychology.'

But to return to the 'gold and silver idol'. This map

showing the Dundon Hill giant squatting in his boat[10]
illustrates better than words how the converging masts of
his ship suggest compasses. A line from the point where
the masts would converge cuts throught the 'Tongue to the
Heart'; it represents the 'chain' or Ray of Light on which
the 'key of St. John's Lodge' depends, for June is St.
John's month.

This statement in the old Masonic Document that the
chain is from the tongue suggests the creative 'Word by
Mouth' of the Logos: the Druids believed 'in the Rays of
Light the vocalization — for one were the hearing and the
seeing'. The Rev. J.W. Ab Ithel in *Druidism* quotes the Roll
of Tradition and Chronology as follows, 'It was from the
vocalization of God's name that every song and music,
vocal or instrumental, were obtained, and every ecstasy,
and every joy, and every life and every felicity, and every
origin and derivation of existence and animation. God
pronounced His name, that is, /|\ ; and with the word all
the worlds and all animation leaped from their origination
into being and life, with a shout of joy. Where and while
the Name of God is kept in memory, in respect of mystery,
number and kind, there cannot but be existence, life,
knowledge and felicity, for ever and ever.'

Herein lies the secret that has been lost so long; it is time
it were recovered, for we read in *The High History* (Branch
VI Title 20) that the Master of the twelve ancient knights
summoneth Messire Gawain 'by word of mouth, and
telleth him that if he delayeth longer, never more will he
recover it'.

That brings us to this Orion being the architect god, not
only because he holds his arm in the form of a square, and
because the 'working tools of a Master Mason' fit him as
demonstrated, but because he is 'the giant who beheld the
three pillars of Light' or the Word, proving him to
represent 'in the earthly Temple of the Stars' a geo-
metrician. 'Thus the working tools of a Master Mason
teach us to bear in mind, and act in accordance with the
laws of our Divine Creator, so that when we shall be
summoned from this sublunary abode we may ascend to
the Grand Lodge above, where the world's Great Architect
lives and reigns for ever.'

The upshot is that *time*, expressed by this zodiac, was the embodiment of all its makers — science, religion and art. Time could not be gauged without the aid of the heavenly bodies; its primary concentrated energy focused in the 'eye of Light' at the meridian, radiating the heavenly compasses by which the circle of 360 degrees could be measured. Astronomers still count the day from noon, being the transit of the mean sun across the meridian, in strict conformity with the rule as to the beginning of the sidereal day.

But there is another effigy to which the converging masts of the boat-of-the-Sun point, as shown on the illustration; it is the Dove. 'From the height of the highest Heaven; a Dove on her flight doth wing, and a Host so white and holy, she unto the stone doth bring.'[11]

This Dove, on whose outstretched wing the well-known stars of the Plough fall, is for that reason the clock of the sky, for the revolution of the Plough stars delineates exactly the 24 hour day; it was thus a token of Time. It also symbolized the Holy Spirit, radiating the 'Unknown Light', the Creative Fire. This Dove is the vehicle of 'The Spiritual Light Principle'.

Sweet brother, I have seen the Holy Grail:
Forwaked at dead of night, I heard a sound
As of a silver horn from o'er the hills and then
Streamed thro' my cell a cold and silver beam.
And down the long beam stole the Holy Grail,
Rose-red with beatings in it, as if alive.

Thus, Tennyson in his 'The Holy Grail' came near to expressing the 'hearing and seeing' of the Ray,

. . . and the slender sound
As from a distance beyond distance grew
Coming upon me — O never harp nor horn,
Was like that music as it came

There is a very considerable literature on the subject of the Quest of the Grail. Scholars such as A.E. Waite have spent their lives seeking and not finding it, probably because they would not see that it was originaly conceived of in the starry universe. Now we know its pictorial setting was laid out on earth in the form of the Zodiacal Circle, the Garden of Eden, the Earthly Paradise according to

Arthurian History. Indeed it is a mistake to jettison that legend, because the snake in the garden has existed for so long, as the constellation Draco in whose toils are concealed the Pole stars; The *High History of the Holy Grail* (Branch XXII Titles 1 and 2), tells us how the castle that belonged to King Fisherman was Eden, and the river that compassed the castle around came from the Earthly Paradise. And again in Wolfram von Eschenbach's Parzival we read, 'Paradise Garden, that thing which men call "The Grail", the crown of all earthly wishes, fair fullness that ne'er shall fail!' 'For the Grail was the crown of blessing, the fullness of earth's delight, and its joys I right well may liken to the glories of Heaven's height!'

So we have found that the 'Master Key' is the manifestation of the Universal, Creative, Divine Mind in the emanating Spark, the original and eternal Idea, for 'the Universe is the Mirror of the Logos'.

> The Hero, quick recalling,
> Speaks the Master words of Knowledge,
> Words that came from distant ages,
> Words his ancestors had taught him.
>
> Finland's 'Kalewala'.

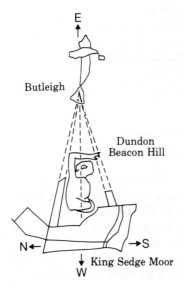

THE DUNDON HILL GIANT

Showing the outline of the effigy Giant, Ship and Bird; with dotted lines superimposed from masts, and tongue of the 'bowed' head.

Scale One-half Inch to One Mile

SIGNS AND SECRETS 6: *Leo*

The celestial lion from China, arrayed in oriental splendour, danced his traditional dance. He wore a magnificent mask of enormous size replete with salmon-pink ears and jade-green eyelids flickering over eyes of pearl that reflected all the colours of the rainbow. His ravening mouth was a masterpiece of expression. At sunrise he was a sleepy lion with lolling head and drowsy eyelids, but at midday a ferocious beast, leaping on his child tamer with cat-like bounds to the beat of metallic drums.

However, this lion is not indigenous to China; it was introduced at the time Buddhism spread east from India, taking along its zodiacal lion, but the queer thing is that the story that goes with it is found in *The High History of the Holy Grail*, (Branch V Titles 1 and 2).

Messire Gawain, like the Chinese hero, is possessed of two swords, one of which is a sacred hallow of the Grail, because it 'inflicted the wound from which the Enchantments of Briton followed'. The child, who in the traditional dance carried the four suns of the four quarters and rode upon the lion after he has tamed him, is the child who, putting his hands together, kneels to Sir Gawain and swears fealty to him, 'And Messire Gawain looketh at the child that rode upon the lion right fainly. "Sir," saith the hermit, "None durst guard him or be master over him save this child only, and yet the lad is not more than six years of age." '

This child was Canis Minor; it will be remembered that in representations of the Chinese Lion-dogs they hold under their paw either a ball (the sun) or a cub. In the Somerset Zodiac the Little Dog lies beneath the paw of Leo, his nose inside the Ecliptic Circle where two of the Gemini stars fall upon it, but his chief star is Procyon in Canis Minor.

If this is the explanation of that star myth, what is the origin of the ring in the lion's mouth, like the one to be seen on the Sanctuary knocker in Gloucester, the history of which was that whoso laid hold of it should be safe. I have in my possession two lion headed Etruscan ear-rings, made of soft reddish gold with a ring pendant from the lower jaw; this is typical, for in many instances along the Mediterranean coast and other regions, the lion is represented with a ring in his mouth, the only explanation being that he thus holds the Ecliptic Circle.

The Lion flames. There the sun's course runs hottest,
When first the sun into the Lion enters.

Aratos

Madame Blavatsky says in the *Secret Doctrine* when speaking of 'the twelve great Orders, recorded in the twelve signs of the zodiac', 'The highest group is composed of the divine Flames, so-called, also spoken of as the "Fiery Lions" and the "Lions of Life", whose esotericism is securely hidden in the Zodiacal sign of Leo. It is the nucleole of the superior divine World,' the "Archetypal World".'

In this Temple of the Stars, the Lion's tongue composed of red clay is one of the most interesting modelled earthworks; it is extended intentionally to rest on and point out the central line of the ecliptic, which corresponds exactly with the accepted Path of the Sun when transferred from the modern planisphere. I marvelled at its lifelike drawing, expressed by the processional path that surrounds it, when I trod in the footsteps of sun worshipping pilgrims, listening to the choirs of birds shouting for joy in the hanging woods above.

The Lion's eye looks along the upper edge of the sun's path, his upraised paw touching the lower edge; certainly no chance arrangement, for just behind Leo, Virgo's Wheat Sheaf is used as a measuring stick to give the same exact width.

The Royal Star Regulus falls on the central line under the tuft of the Lion's tail, which no doubt is the reason why 'his tail turned up over his back' in star maps and heraldry. One of the most interesting references to the Somerset Lion is in a very ancient note in William of Malmesbury's *Antiquities of Glastonbury* (F. Lomax's translation published by Talbot) which says 'that miracles should not cease until the great lion had come,

having a tail fastened with great chains. Again, in what
follows concerning the search for a cup which is there
called the Holy Grail, the same is related almost at the
beginning.' Those chains fastening the lion's tail are
Christian's Cross, which is the place-name marked on the
map of the cross roads holding the tuft on his tail, where a
cross used to stand, probably marking the spot that
indicated the fall of the summer solstice when the Temple
was laid out.

Alcott, in *Star Lore of All Ages*, says, 'Many authorities
claim it is beyond question that the place of the sun at the
summer solstice was in this constellation at the time when
the star groups were designed. There was thus a visible
connection between the constellation Leo and the return of
the sun to the place of power and glory at the apex of the
heavenly arch.'

According to Greek mythology, Leo is the Nemean lion,
which, after being killed by Hercules, was raised to the
heavens by Jupiter in honour of Hercules.

The effigies speak for themselves; who would have
believed that more than 4000 years ago the astronomers
deduced the exact position of the solstitial and equinoctial
cross at the time of the layout of the Temple, or the exact
position and width of the ecliptic according to modern
planispheres, and had the knowledge to reduce the whole
chart of the Universe to the proportions of this 'Paradise
Garden'! So it is important to point out the forceful and
obviously intentional gestures of the effigies in order to
verify what is known by geometrical and astronomical
proofs. For instance, another gesture of note is that of the
Giant Orion grasping the imaginary central line of the
ecliptic with his upraised right hand; probably the origin
of the Sanctuary knocker legend whosoever lays hold of
the pathway of the sun-god must be saved.

Before leaving the subject of the lion's tail with its tuft
hanging over the Royal Star Regulus, let us pause to
apprehend the humorous point of view of the twelfth
century romancer in respect to it. Virgo 'the damsel seeth
above the altar (i.e. the star Regulus) the most holy cloth
for the which she was come thither, that was right ancient,
and a smell came thereof so sweet and glorious that no

sweetness of the world might equal it. The damsel cometh toward the altar thinking to take the cloth, but it goeth up into the air as if the wind had lifted it. Forthwith the cloth came down above the altar, and she straightway found taken away therefrom as much as it pleased Our Lord she should have. Joseph telleth us of a truth, that never did none enter into the chapel that might touch the cloth save only this one damsel.' Which is manifest, if one looks at Virgo's position in star pictures! In India it was customary to bury a lock of hair under the foundations of a new Temple, in the belief that the life as well as the spirit of its owner (in this case that of the Lion) should enter into the Temple. Virgo was certainly the first 'tuft-hunter'

In the Romano British burial ground on the Lion's tail I myself handled many lion's claws that had been buried with the sun worshippers, probably holding the same idea, for in Freemasonry it is the Lion's Grip that raises the spiritually dead to life, a very ancient landmark traceable back to Palestine and Egypt, for the lion is almost exclusively associated with the regenerating power of the sun, and hence with resurrection. *The High History of the Holy Grail* describes this 'Graveyard Perilous' in Branch XV Titles 14-21.

We found in the graves large flat stones cut in the form of wheels, for the Sun god at the solstice was metaphorically crucified on the Solar Wheel, which, like the cross, is a stone age as well as a Chaldean symbol. The memory of these sun symbols is found in many customs perpetuated in England, such as rolling blazing wheels down hill sides and flaming tar barrels along the streets, or dancing round the Maypole. As all these customs were kept up for hundreds of years in the immediate neighbourhood of the Lion, it is interesting to see Maypole Knap still writ large upon his left paw on the map.

Around this paw clusters what was once the capital town of Somerset. Now Somerset is the early form of somersault, i.e., a wheel turned in the air and Somerton, the original capital town, marks for all time the summer months of July and August on this zodiacal calendar.

The wheel on top of the Maypole symbolizes the circle of the ecliptic, the primary purpose of the dancers being the revolution of the sun, whilst the coloured streamers represent rays; so it is the rotary movement of these wheels that constitutes the solar symbolism. Not only is it a nature fertility rite, but an excellent example of sympathetic magic, so called, for at all costs the sun must run its course through the zodiacal constellations once in twenty-four hours, or the calendrical calculations would be confounded with universal chaos! According to this idea the more the May or Midsummer dancers danced round the Pole in sympathy with the universe the more fertile Mother Nature would be.

All magic is based on the law of sympathy — that is the assumption that things act on one another at a distance because of their being secretly linked together by invisible bonds, which would account for the laying out of the star effigies on earth. I have no doubt, when conceived, this Paradise Garden was indeed heaven on earth; even now, those who understand its import cannot but be filled with wonder, awe and reverence, for it is the cradle of the Holy Grail, the inspiration of true Knighthood, 'a magic casement opening on the foam of perilous seas, in faery lands forlorn'.

The tribe of Judah, and King Arthur with the kings of England, took for their banner this Lion of the Sun, and the old Roman College of Architects or Comacine Masons from whom the Freemasons were directly descended carved the Lion as their symbol. He was invoked in Egypt as the Supreme God, and whether spoken of as Ra or Osiris he was constantly addressed as 'The God in Lion Form', Osiris the Lion of Yesterday, Ra the Lion of Tomorrow; also the two lions are two solar phases, diurnal and nocturnal, and as there is but one solar orb, so he is the lion of the double lions.

In the funeral ritual, the Osirian or soul seeking divine union and communion with the sun god prays: 'Let me not be surpassed by the Lion god; Oh, the Lion of the Sun, who lifts his arm in the hill and exclaims: I am the Lions I am the Sun.'

I shall never forget my utter amazement when the truth dawned on me, that the outline of a lion was drawn by the curves of the Cary River below the old capital town of

Somerset. So that was the origin of the legendary lion that I had been questing! A nature effigy, and a god of sun-worshippers! Leo of the zodiac. As Wolfram von Eschenbach wrote in his Parzival A.D. 1170, 'Tis rich in all earthly riches, yet he who that castle fair would seek, he may never find it, tho many that quest shall dare. Unawares must they chance upon it, for I wat in no other wise shall that Burg and all that it holdeth be looked on by mortal eyes.' Obviously, if the lion was a nature effigy then the dragon, griffon, and the giants etc., must also be; this was the most thrilling moment of my discovery.

SIGNS AND SECRETS 7: *Virgo*

'Queen of the Earth who there appears,
inclining graciously to all.'

Virgo of the Round Table of the Stars in Somerset holds a
long-kept secret; she stands for the month of September
and the date of the Blessed Virgin Mary's birthday falls in
September. This fact explains the origin of such dogmas as
the immaculate conception and other such tenets held for
hundreds of years by her devotees and still taken on trust
by Roman Catholics; as applied to this Mother Earth,
always she is being fecundated, conceives and brings forth
without being defiled.

She has perhaps the most interesting history of any of
these archaic constellation effigies. The old Greek
describes the Virgin Mother thus:
Divine Mother of the ALL,
Chaste nourisher of men.
Bounteous giver, Demeter!
Nourisher of corn, giver of all,
Delighted by the works of peace
And of diligent labour.
Queen of the Earth who there appears,
Inclining graciously to all,
Prolific, friend of children,
Chaste Virgin, nourisher of men!
Goddess sublime of mortal men,
Many forms hast thou
Resplendent, glorious, holy!
Come, thou blessed One, ever-pure,
Laden with summer's fruits:
Bring us the peace and order of love,
Richness, abundance of blessing,
And health, O Thou Queen!
Virgo's fertile lands in the Kingdom of Logres are guarded
by the famous castle of Arthurian romance, Camelot. On
modern maps the fort is called Cadbury Castle, but the
river flowing from it still retains the name of Cam, with

Queen Camel on its banks, and many maps name 'King Arthur's Hunting Causeway,' that leads from the castle towards Virgo's effigy and Glastonbury. Castle Cary used also to guard it from the East. Tennyson sang:

Arthur's ancient seat which made the Briton's name thro' all the world so great.

Like Camelot, what place was ever yet renowned? Where as at Caerleon oft, he kept the Table Round.

Camulos was a sky god and the mountain in Palestine called Carmel was itself a god and known as 'the garden of God'. Godfrey Higgins says in his *Anacalypsis*, 'The Carmelites are in a very peculiar manner attached to the worship of the Virgin Mary, more particularly than any of the other monastic orders ... In the book of the office of the Carmelites, Mary is called Maris Stella, Mother of our Maker, and the glorious Virgin of Mount Carmel. She has forty-three names.' We will return to Maris Stella presently, but first let us look at Virgo's effigy, reclining on her side amongst her wheat fields, as Queen of heaven and earth.

Perhaps the best view of the Virgin's outline is to be obtained from Castle Cary's castle hill, whence the Cary River, rising in the spring called Our Lady, can be seen meandering around the folds of her flowing robes to her breast, called Wimble Toot, meaning augur's teat.[1] (This so called 'tumulus' is now fortunately preserved as a National Monument.) Then from her breast the river continues its course round her sleeve, to outline in profile, her beautiful throat and face decked in a high bonnet.

Traced on the map one can see where the old fairy tale got its idea of the witch riding on a broomstick, for she holds outstretched a sheaf of wheat, her 'kern-baby', in order that the sun can bless it in his course round the ecliptic circle, it being the exact width of his imaginary path. The star in Virgo that marks 20 September on the planisphere falls on the centre of this wheat sheaf.

It was pointed out in *A Guide to Glastonbury's Temple of the Stars* that the male characters of Arthurian Romance impersonate the star constellations, whilst the women represent the rivers and springs of this 'Paradise Garden'. Parzival's sister is the Cary River which outlines

the effigy Virgo, whilst his mother is this effigy, the
famous 'widow lady', 'Welsh Queen of two lands' (see
Hertzeleide). Her husband, whose ancestor was Mazadan,
according to Wolfram von Eschenbach, was first married
to a Moorish Queen and their son, half brother to Parzival,
was 'black and white'. The English term 'Black-a-Moor'
means black as a Moor.

The Spaniards always had a strong strain of Arab
blood, and in the seventh century North Africa and the
peninsula were again overrun by the Moors; thus we are
told the first cousin of Parzival's father was 'king of
Spain', as well he might be. King Sedge Moor, through
which the Cary River finds its way to the Severn, is termed
a Sea Moor.

The Saracens and Moors are often referred to in the
Arthurian legends; 'ethnically they are a hybrid race with
more Arab than Berber blood', but it is a very interesting
fact that the skulls dug up, of the inhabitants of the
Glastonbury Lake villages, 'all belong to the oval headed
Mesaticephalic' type. According to Sir William Boyd
Dawkin's findings, 'they are physically identical with the
small dark inhabitants of the Basque Provinces of Spain
and the Berber. The same race occurs in Asia Minor.' This
again bears out the theory that the makers of the Somerset
Zodiac came from that region.

Before we leave Castlecaryland, let us gaze at the
enchanted bay to the west, 500 feet below, where lies the
Vessel of the Holy Grail. It may be lapped by waves of
mist beating in from the Severn Sea, called the White Lady
of Sedge Moor. If so, the hills that form the Phoenix, the
Archer's horse, the Lion, the Giant Twin, the Ram and the
Fish, will float like islands half concealed in her embrace,
but often the whole sacred area is bathed in the blood of a
tremendous sunset, and then the old gods appear to seethe
in their mystic 'cauldron.

And now to return to the Virgin's secret. *The Journal of
Calendar Reform* for December, 1936, published an interesting article by the Abbe Chauve-Bertrand entitled
'Origins of Christmas', concerning the conception, birth
and death of Christ. As the Abbe is such an authority on
the subject of the Calendar one quotes him as one would

an encyclopaedia. When about the fourth century we are told, 'the Feast of the Nativity' took root in Rome, 'nobody was in a position to prove that the event had taken place on 25 December', for 'there is no tradition concerning the date of the birth of Christ.' So 25 March was chosen symbolically for His death, and 27 March for His Resurrection. His conception was given as the spring equinox and consequently 25 December for his birth.

I might suggest that the clue to the dilemma was the spring equinox in March, for the sun had moved out of the stars of the Lamb, Aries, marking April, into the stars of the Fish, Pisces, and in the new calendar the vernal equinox had been adjusted: the sun at the autumnal equinox lay in the stars of Virgo.

The Abbe favours the winter solstice as the real reason for the choice of 25 December for the birthday of the Saviour; he remarks upon the opposition of 'Christ, the Spiritual Sun, to the pagan sun god', and says, hence 'the practice of counteracting the pagan ceremony with a Christian solemnity in which was celebrated the birth of the One who was presented as the true Sun'. He adds that the Arabs and others 'had the custom of taking from a sanctuary, at the time of the winter solstice, an idol of the sun, represented as a new born child, whilst the priest went along and chanted the following: "Korah, the Virgin, has given birth to Aion." Aion was the new sun ... To get to the bottom of this explanation it remains to be said who this celestial virgin was. She was simply the one whose name figures in the signs of the Zodiac. . . . Now, after the harvest season, the stars of the Virgo Constellation descend slowly. When they disappeared on the horizon, the sun, at the winter solstice, was placed as though in the bosom and was born, so to say, in the arms of the celestial virgin at the heliacal rising on the eastern horizon; it was he who, in this guise was represented as a child nursed by a chaste virgin, in the astrological picture of the wise men of Persia', and again, 'Let no one be frightened by all this. . . . We do not realize fully how much the liturgies owe to astronomy.'

Since 'truth will out', even though kept secret for nearly two thousand years, need I say more except to cap this

with another from the twelfth century, which will bring it
down to earth. Wolfram von Eschenbach in his Parzival,
Book IX relates, concerning 'a wonder God wrought from
the earth and clay.'

Quoth Parzival, 'Now I think me that never such thing
might be,

And 'twere better thou shouldst keep silent, than tell
such a tale to me!

For who should have borne the father, whose son, as
thou sayest, reft,

Maidenhood, from his father's mother? Such riddle were
better left!'

But the hermit again made answer, 'Now thy doubt will
I put away,

O'er my falsehood thou canst bemoan thee if the thing
be not truth I say,

For the EARTH was Adam's mother, of the EARTH was
Adam fed,

And I ween, tho' a man she bare here, yet still was the
Earth a maid.'

'Nor on earth shall aught be purer than a maiden
undefiled,

Think how pure must be a maiden, since God was a
Maiden's Child!

Two men have been born of maidens, and God hath the
likeness taken

Of the son of the first Earth-Maiden, since to help us He
aye was fain.'

'From the lips of the whole world's Lover came a
message of love, and peace,

For He is a Light all-lightening, and never His faith
doth cease.'

Religions, the world over, have worshipped the Sun
Father-god and the Earth Virgin-mother at some time
during their history, with the natural corollary that the
father had to be born from the stellar Virgo first!

To observe that the Sun was apparently born in the
bosom of the constellation Virgo, at the winter solstice,
necessitated hundreds of years of stellar observation. In
order to perpetuate and fix for all time their vision of the
constellations, 'the first men of the east, who brought it to

the west', drew the starry Mother of the Harvest, that they had envisaged, upon the earth in Somerset, England; or rather they found her there already outlined by the Cary River, and all they had to do was to add her breast and her bouquet of wheat.[2] This we know because when the modern planisphere is traced on the map of the Sacred Area, some of the stars of Virgo fall upon her wheat-sheaf in the same way that the stars of the other zodiacal creatures fall on their corresponding counterparts.

'Hail to the dove, the restorer of Light'

The Isle of Avalon rims the northern side of Somerset's Stellar Circle, Glastonbury Tor forming a partly natural pyramid above it, and there, according to historical records, King Arthur's tomb was marked in the Abbey graveyard, by a Pyramid. But before he 'passed' into this famous Isle where the Sun was thought to hibernate, he met Mordred.

The Persians called the month of November 'Mordred', meaning 'the angel of death', and that month marked the festival of death in many other lands, as it still does amongst Freemasons. So the 17th day of Athyr was no doubt the day that Mordred chose to mortally wound King Arthur 'on the side of his head', for Malory recounts, in his *Morte D'Arthur*, 'There was a day assigned betwixed King Arthur and Sir Mordred that they should meet upon a down beside Salisbury, and not far from the seaside'. This 'down' is on the direct high road to Scorpio's effigy, which lies in the Vale of Avalon to which vale the weeping Queens took Arthur after he was wounded.

As the stars of both Scorpio and Serpens fall on this giant effigy, marking the month of November, the text continues, 'right soon came an adder (venomous snake) out of a little heath bush ... and then was King Arthur ware where Sir Mordred leaned upon his sword among a great heap of dead men.' However, though wounded, the King kills his arch enemy, for as we shall see he vanquished death, the sun god's spirit — according to the Druids — escaping in the form of a bird, from his head.

Now Plutarch stated of Osiris that he was disposed of 'the 17th day of the month Athor, when the sun was in Scorpio', and that 'the first who knew of the accident which had befallen their king, were the Pans and Satyrs.' As part of December is 'ruled over' by the goat sign Capricornus, it explains why Pans and Satyrs were the first to bemoan the fate of nature's king.

All sun-gods rise again, hence the saying 'King Arthur

will return', and in celebrating the mystic rites of Adonis (which rites were much the same as those of Hercules) 'after the attendants had for a long time bewailed the death of this just person, he was at length understood to be restored to life, to have experienced a resurrection, signified by the readmission of light. On this the priest addressed the company, saying "Comfort yourselves, all ye have been partakers of the mysteries of Deity, thus preserved." The people answered by the invocation "Hail to the Dove!" the Restorer of Light!'

The Egyptians as well as the Druids believed that the soul escaped after death in the form of a bird, so let us turn from the Scorpion of death to the Air Sign Libra, which he indicates by pointing with his great claw on which the stars of Libra fall, to the Dove; for it is remarkable that hovering over the head of the Archer sun-god (Arthur), in this Somerset Zodiac, is the Dove with outstretched wing pointing to the 'Secret Sanctuary that gives upon the Earthly Paradise'.

This bird is designed to fit the effigy body from which it has escaped, for one wing is half closed like the bent arm of the Archer, the other extended, and the tail is at the same angle as the hips; thus the Dove has slipped out of the body of the Sun-god, like a snake out of its skin.

From the spiritual standpoint of Arthurian drama, the Dove has the most important part to play. Mr. A.E. Waite says in his *Holy Grail,* 'In the prose Lancelot, which prefaces the great and glorious Quest the Pageant has this characteristic — that it is preceded invariably by a Dove, bearing a golden censer in its beak, and the Palace fills thereupon with the eternal sweetness of Paradise which is above. The bird passes through the Hall and out of sight into a Chamber beyond. From that Chamber — as if at a concerted signal — or almost as if the Dove had suffered transformation — there issues the Maiden of the Grail, carrying the Precious Vessel.'

This Dove can be traced with the aid of the map, on the still unspoiled fields around Barton St. David; that it forms part of the ancient landmarks of the Temple area there can be no doubt, because as in the case of the other effigies, the Grail legends confirm the archaeological findings.

Dr. S.A. Ionides states that in Wales, 'according to the chroniclers, the Great Bear of the sky, who describes a Circle round the Pole and never sets, is the true originator of Sir Arthur Pendragon's famous Round Table'. The connection also lay in this effigy Dove upon which the stars of the Great Bear do fall, and which was called King Arthur's Chariot by the Druids and Irish, meaning the vehicle of his spirit, 'the Restorer of Light'.

So here is proof that our ancestors, 5,000 years ago, believed that the spirit left the body at death and flew to Heaven in the semblance of a dove, still the symbol of the Holy Ghost in the Church of today. If circumstantial evidence is needed for the survival of this prehistoric tradition it will be found on page 460 of Dr. Axel Munthe's book *The Story of San Michele*. He tells of the custom in Capri (that island in the bay of Naples) of trapping birds in order to let them loose in the Church at Easter, which he says is 'their way of celebrating the resurrection of our Lord, consecrated by the tradition of nearly two thousand years and still encouraged by their priests. From the first day of Holy Week the traps had been set in every vineyard, under every olive tree ... symbols of the Holy Dove, they were to be set free in the church to play their role in the jubilant commemoration of Christ's return to Heaven.'

Wolfram von Eschenbach[1] tells us that every Good Friday the white dove came from 'the height of the highest Heaven' to bring to earth 'all good that on earth may be', 'as the fullness of Paradise'; in token of which the Grail Knights and their horses wore the white dove given to them by the King of the Grail, Anfortas. It is a well known Templar symbol.

Few can doubt that here in Somerset is indeed 'the First Church of Britain'[2] as has so often been stated but never properly understood, and at the same time 'A Heavenly Sanctuary on Earth'. In Welsh mythology this Vale of Avalon (according to the Encyclopaedia) was looked upon as 'the kingdom of the dead, afterwards an earthly paradise in the western seas, and finally, in the Arthurian romances, the abode of heroes to which King Arthur was conveyed after his last battle.'

It is appropriate at the end to tell of the north east quarter
of the Somerset circle, for the sun of the old year awaits his
rebirth on 25 December like King Arthur who vanished in
the Vale of Avalon, where his effigy lies. The young
Canadian poet Audrey Brown, in a lovely poem, has
caught the strange remoteness of the place thus —
   Arthur of Avalon
   Spoke from the dew-cold turf where he was lying:
   'Surely the night is gone:
   I hear a tumult as of bugles crying
   Out of the blood-red east. — Ah harken, harken!
   The sword and shield are met:
   I will go forth!' — But still with eyes a-darken,
   She answered him — 'Not yet'!'
for the legend is that he will return at the time of his
country's greatest need.
   The better to understand let us turn to *Ancient Art and
Ritual* by Jane Harrison, 'Osiris stands as the prototype of
the great class of resurrection-gods who die that they may
live again'; she goes on to say that a Mystery-play was
enacted every year at Abydos in ancient Egypt, symbolizing the death, burial and resurrection of Osiris in the
'Garden' of the god, which seems to have been a large pot;
herein was planted the effigy of Osiris and also barley
which when watered grew, 'for the growth of the garden is
the growth of the divine substance'. At Philae a representation of this shows ears of corn sprouting out of his body:
and at Dendera the god himself comes to life, for in a
beautiful basrelief he is carved rising out of the bowl or
garden.
   Nothing could give a better idea than the above of the
meaning of the vast Garden of the Grail in Somerset,
which lies near the mouth of the Severn River.
   The *Light of Britannia* (page 114) states, 'In Welsh, the
West of England is still called the country of the Goat
because it borders on the Severn, which seems to have
been sacred to both the old Sun of the dying year and the
infant Sun of the new year.' The Goat is the Goat-fish, one
of the zodiacal effigies in this Garden who was wet nurse

to Zeus, Sun-god like Hercules.

The Druid tradition held that Hercules went into a fish where he continued part of three days and three nights. When he came out again he had lost his hair and appeared as a beardless babe; he was in the fish from 20 to 22 December, and Hercules was said to be born at the winter solstice, which lay in front of the nose of the Goat-fish when the Temple of the Stars was laid out.

Here and now we can answer the Kabalistic question on the subject of the Sun-cross, found in Vol. II of *The Secret Doctrine*, 'The theoretical use of crucifixion must have been somehow connected with the personification of this symbol (the structure of the garden of Paradise symbolized by a crucified man). But how and as showing what? The symbol was of the origin of measures, shadowing forth creative law or design. What practically, as regards humanity, could actual crucifixion betoken? Yet, that it was held as the effigy of some mysterious working of the same system, is shown from the very fact of the use.' Yes indeed, for in this garden of Paradise, Hercules lies outlined in the form of a cross, his arms outstretched like the Archer drawing his bow, his eye looking straight along the equinoctial line that falls parallel with them, when drawn between the places of the Royal Stars Aldebaran and Antares. This sight line cuts through the exact Centre of the Somerset Circle, to which Hercules points, thus confirming for all time the date of its construction, when the Royal Stars suggested the Sun-Cross. And more than that, he is the dying Sun-god of the old year crucified on the winter solstice or Christmas tree. So it is quite true that 'the symbol was of the origin of measures, shadowing forth creative law or design'.

Madame Blavatsky says on the preceding page, '"To crucify before the sun" is a phrase used of initiation. It comes from Egypt and primarily from India. The initiated adept, who had successfully passed through all the trials, was tied on a cross, in deep sleep, and allowed to remain in that state for three days and three nights, during which time his Spiritual Ego was said to confabulate with the "gods", descend into Hades, Amenti, etc: (according to the country). At a certain hour the beam of the rising Sun

struck full on the face of the entranced candidate, and like
Hercules he was born again.'

Witness the passage in Malory's *Le Morte D'Arthur;* just
before the 'passing' into the Vale of Avalon, 'King Arthur
dreamed a wonderful dream, and that was this: that him
seemed he sat upon a chaflet in a chair, and the chair was
fast to a Wheel, and thereupon sat King Arthur in the
richest cloth of gold that might be made; and the king
thought there was under him, a deep black water,
andtherein were all manner of serpents, and wild beasts;
and suddenly the king thought the wheel turned up-so-
down, and he fell among the serpents, and every beast
took him by a limb'. Thus this solar hero dropped down in
Somerset amongst the zodiacal beasts and Draco (the
serpent whose head he cut off) — he 'descended into Hades
to confabulate with the gods.' We are told that it happened
when 'King Arthur drew him down by the sea side
Westward'.

La Queste del Saint Graal describes his Round Table as
a Wheel, 'After that table there was another like it.... That
was the Table of the Holy Graal[1] which gave rise to so
many and great miracles in this country... Now, fair Sire,
in the meadow which you saw there was a rack. By this
rack we must understand the Round Table, for just as in
the rack there are spindles which separate the compart-
ments, so in the Round Table there are pillars which
separate the seats.' And this so-called Table fed 150 bulls
and 4,000 people.

One of the beasts that holds the Sun King 'by a limb', is
the Goat; the illustration shows that the lower part of his
right leg is hidden behind its head, his knee next to its
horn; that also tallies with the Greek myth that the horn of
the Goat nourished Zeus, 'in the horn Cornucopia was
found all that could be desired of flowers and fruit'. Zeus
placed the horn together with the goat amongst the stars.
The immense horn, measuring five-eigths of a mile long
and twenty-one feet high, after nearly 5,000 years of wear
and tear and archaeological excavation still grows 'all
that could be desired of flowers and fruit', and once upon a
time the Sun itself lodged therein at the winter solstice.
This horn of Capricornus, called Ponters Ball, lies just

below Glastonbury Tor. I remember the old farmer who lived by it telling me that its real name was 'the Golden Coffin though nobody knew why', but the Druids knew that the Sun-god lay in this Goat's Golden Coffin when he dismounted from his horse. The December stars fall on the Somerset Hercules effigy, if transferred from the planisphere to the map of the area; and the stars of the first and second months of the New Year fall on the Goat effigy during which time the infant Sun is being suckled by his nurse.

Dr. Waddell in his *Phoenician Origin* gives several illustrations of the goat in connection with Hercules, remarking 'The Goat is figured freely on Sumerian and Hitto-Phoenician seals from the earliest period, and also on Early Briton monuments and coins associated with the Sun Cross, which explains the fact of the Goat being still the mascot of the Welsh Cymri.'

Herodotus tells us Hercules was merely a canonized human hero, thus analogous to St. George and King Arthur, but Dr. Waddell goes further and proves he was originally Gilgamesh.

In a previous chapter I have pointed out at some length that Gilgamesh (Marduk) was responsible for the design and scientific ordering of the Zodiacal Circle, according to the Epic of Gilgamesh preserved in the British Museum. Can it be that the magnificently drawn figure of Hercules, outlined in the Vale of Avalon, is none other than that of its first law giver Gilgamesh?

It will be remembered it was the death of his friend, Enkidu, that sent him on his intrepid visit to the netherworld to find him, and this friend was the Goat, for the first Tablet, after saying he was modelled out of clay, relates, 'His body was covered all over with hair, the hair of his head was long like that of a woman, and he wore clothing like that of the god of cattle. He was different in every way from people of the country, and his name was Enkidu. He lived in the forests on the hills, ate herbs like the gazelle, drank with wild cattle, and herded with the beasts of the field. He was mighty in stature, invincible in strength'. In fact Enkidu resembles in many other respects the later god Pan, who took the shape of the Goat-fish during the 'War of the Giants', for which reason Jupiter put him in heaven.

There is a good deal more behind this Earth sign than first appears, witness the 10th Tarot Trump card, 'The Wheel of Fortune', which belongs to Capricornus, but we will let John Rhys sum up for us, 'Here we have also a horned beast older than Zeus. This would, however, not be any answer to the question whence the idea of a horned god of the nether world was derived; one might, for example, look for it in a still cruder manner of regarding him not only as the first offspring of time, but also as the first in point of order in space — that is, as the foundation and upholder of the mass of the universe.' (See Hibbert Lecture on the *Origin and Growth of Religion as illustrated by Celtic Heathendom.*)

The realization of these gigantic forms of the ancient gods, looming out of the mists of ages, is immensely impressive and awe inspiring. Creatures of Time, lying under 'the dew-cold turf', not in any haphazard circle, but literally based on complex geometrical figures, and corresponding with their celestial counterparts. Colossal sculptures planned by astronomer architects, and modelled by nature sculptors of a remotely innocent age. Silent, utterly forgotten, all memory of their existence wilfully destroyed, and yet they are the prototype of zodiacal charts still in use at the present time, that even today preserve their salient characteristics, though none of the astonomical historians have been able to find out the existence of the original! Since its discovery it has been said, 'there is nothing of archaeological importance to compare with this earth work Circle of zodiacal effigies, not even the Great Pyramid.'

So at long last I found that the vessel of the Holy Grail was in the beginning the tomb in this garden of our destiny, but the 'tree of life' springs out of it, the stars for fruit. The vitalizing rays of the 'true Sun' are caught in this cauldron of our universe and all creation is redeemed.

Here is the symbolic tomb of 'the mysteries' leading to resurrection and eternal life; a message down the ages, 'As from beyond the limit of the world. Like the last echo born of a great cry.' I AM THE CELL, I AM THE OPENING CHASM, I AM THE PLACE OF RE-ANIMATION.

AN APPRECIATION
Philip S. Wellby

The claim that the mystical fane of Glastonbury is a pre-Christian zodiacal Temple, comparable in grandeur with Stonehenge, finds support in a remarkable work of which the following is an appreciation.

We have been fools, and we must pay therefore
With this dull life, and labor very sore
Until we die; yet we are grown too wise
Upon the earth to seek for paradise.

William Morris

The admission 'we have been fools' is not rare amongst men today. Some may recall the days of infancy when tales of kings and knights, of lions and dragons, of high adventure and strange enchantments, beguiled the heart. Some too may have been content in later years to prolong their sojourn in childhood's realms in company with Malory or other ancient chronicles; to these the legends of King Arthur and *The High History of the Holy Graal* served as spacious regions for tireless wanderings that found their goal in the island valley of Avalon. But even those fortunate ones confessed secretly to the vanity of their dreams of such a Paradise:

For folk of ours bearing the memory
Of our old land, in days past oft have striven
To reach it, unto none of whom was given
To come again and tell us of the tale.

Yet at this very moment in time, when one may voyage to far Cathay by air, or surmount the fabled mountains of the Moon, there comes news of wonders as great as any we have known, lying close at our doors and open to discovery. Here, at my hand, lies a guide to the Temple of the Stars. In the heart of Somerset the reader may gaze upon Merlin's Round Table of the Graal in the valleys of Avalon, hard by the 'Moors adventurous'.

In a part of Somerset which now enfolds the towns of Somerton and Glastonbury was this wondrous temple constructed, 'not without great significance, upon the advice of Merlin', as we may read in *La Questa del Saint Graal.*

Some five thousand years ago there came to this land those who had learned all that Egypt or Chaldea could teach them of the cosmic plane of the sun's journey through the zodiacal constellations as observed from the earth, of the Giant Orion, of Regulus and Antares, Aldebaran and Fomalhaut. Their needs were few, for they were sustained by that most ancient of the Grails, the Cauldron of Wisdom, the mystic cauldron of unfailing supply and the magic cup of healing.

In this land these great emissaries designed and constructed the Temple of the Stars, ten miles in diameter, in which were delineated by the contours of the land, by streams and forest, by tracks and earthworks, 'enormous effigies resembling zodiacal creatures arranged in a circle', Leo, Virgo, Scorpio, and the rest of the twelve 'signs', corresponding with those configurations in the heavens, and following their circular sequence, an inverted panorama of the celestial plan, drawn out 'in such a way as to resemble the dome of heaven inverted on ' Such a temple, by the nature of its construction, could only be destroyed by seismic convulsion, or by a force sufficiently powerful to alter the configuration of the chosen site.

In the main it has escaped such injury, and has endured to this day.

Many changes have been witnessed by the Temple of the Stars; the hills have been occupied by many races in succession, by the Goidels or Celts, by Britons, by Belgae from Northern France (200 B.C.), by the all-conquering Romans, and finally (A.D. 733) by the Saxons.

Providence ordained that those who formed the first church in Britain should inherit the land of the prehistoric zodiacal temple, 'a heavenly sanctuary on earth' as William of Malmesbury describes it. Those who had been initiated into the mysteries of this 'island valley' were obliged to couch their secret knowledge in romance after Christianity swept the field, but the monks of Glastonbury doubtless 'had the whole history thereof true from the beginning even to the end', as *The High History* tells us.

Although the romance *Perceval le Gallois*, translated by Sebastian Evans into English, casts a medieval veil over the pre-Christian Celestial Temple of the Mysteries, it is possible, as the author has proved, to reconstruct it from the text by the aid of modern maps, which display the whole plan to the eye of the reader, and enable him to observe the close correspondence between the effigies on the earth and their celestial counterparts.

The scholarly archaeologist to whom we owe this alluring work[1] has drunk deeply the cup of Nature's oldest vintage — life-memories.

It is consoling to find that it is not entirely vanity 'upon the earth to seek for Paradise'.

FOREWORD
1. *The High History of the Holy Grail*, trans Sebastian Evans, published by James Clarke & Co.

CHAPTER 1
1. The second 'Mighty Labour' was Stonehenge: see Williams' *Ecclesiastical Antiquities of the Cymry*, chpt 8.
2. Plunket, *Ancient Calendars and Constellations*, 1903. On the Roman zodiac Aquarius was represented by a peacock.
3. Ibid.
4. See Lewis Spence, *The Mysteries of Britain*, p.121.
5. See John Rhys's 'Hibbert Lectures' (1886).
6. Edward Davies, *The Mythology and Rites of the British Druids*, 1809, pp.295-99.
7. See Rev. John William ab Ithel, *Druidism*, 1871. The science of Hu the Mighty was preserved by the wise men of the nation of the Cymry and he was the first to lead the Cymry over into the Isle of Britain from the Summer country. The creative Name of Light was recovered to memory whilst the Cymry were still in the East. Dr Waddell says, in his *Origin of Britons and Scots*, p.190: 'We discover that the "Cymry" of Wales derive their name from "Sumer". This latter was a term occasionally used by the early ruling race in Babylonia, the Sumerians of modern Assyriologists.' The First Triad says: 'There was no tribute paid to any but to the race of the Cymry because they first possessed the Isle of Britain.' The Sixth Triad, supplementing this, says: 'First Hu Gardarn originally conducted the nation of the Cymry into the Isle of Britain. They came from the Summer Country over the hazy sea.'
8. Nutt, *The Legend of the Holy Grail*.
9. The Alexandrian Zodiac is said not to have contained the Balance, and its place was occupied by the Scorpion's claws. See Drummond, *Oedipus Judaicus* (1811). Of the Scorpion, Ovid says:
    In the wide circuit of the heavens he shines
        And fills the place of two zodiacal signs.
10. Edward Hutton, *Highways and Byways of Somerset*.
11. Delta was called Wasat, 'the Middle', by the Arabians.
12. Lewis Spence, *The Mysteries of Britain*, p.191
13. See Rev. John William ab Ithel, *Druidism*, p.7, and Geoffrey of Monmouth's *History of the Kings of Britain*, p.14. See also Schliemann's *Troja* and the British Museum's 'Bronze Age Guide'. Hissarlik, the first city of Troy, belonged to the Mycenean age and the dawn of the bronze age, which agrees with the date of our findings in Somerset. Apart from history, Sir Hercules Read, speaking for the British Museum, said: 'Bronze torcs are common in the south west of England. A clue to their date is given in a gold torc which was found by Schliemann in the royal treasure of the second city of the hill of Hissarlik, which preceded the Homeric city of Troy by about a thousand years.' Both Canon Greenwell and Sir Arthur Evans drew attention to the 'Owl Face of Hissarlik' dated 2700 B.C. which reached Britian on such objects as the chalk drums belonging to the early age of metal. Many archaeological relics as well as tradition and folklore throw light upon the ancient landmarks of this Temple of the Stars.
14. Quoted from Geoffrey of Monmouth's *History of the Kings of Britain*. Milton says: 'These verses, originally Greek, were put in Latin (saith Virunnius), by Gildas, a British poet, and him to have liv'd under Claudius.'

CHAPTER 2
1. Maspero, *The Dawn of Civilization*, 'Egypt and Chaldea', p.545.
2. 'Nimrod, of Belus, was judge of the Cushen.' See G. D. Barber, *Ancient Oral Records of the Cimri or Britons* (1855).
3. See Knight and Butter's 'Crest Book', plates K.1 and M.10: compare the jewel of the H.R.A. and also the thigh bones crossed on the Knights Templar Charm with my articles on 'Gemini' and 'the Word'.

CHAPTER 3
1. See Wallis Budge, *Amulets and Superstitions*, p.392 for an illustration of the five-pronged Kabalistic symbol.

CHAPTER 5
1. Dr Waddell, *British Edda*, traces them to Urd, i.e. Carchemish.
2. Alcott, *Star Lore of all Ages*, p.118.

CHAPTER 6
1. Amongst the many legends of this calf in England, a 'golden calf' was said to have been kept in the church at Montacute, and was later sent to Glastonbury.

PART II
INTRODUCTION
1. The Round Table instituted by Joseph in imitation of the Holy Supper was called 'Graal' in the Romance of Merlin: see Hargrave Jennings.

CHAPTER 1: Aquarius
1. Nennius, *Historia Brittonum*, A.D. 800. Arthur's son was also said to have been buried in the Isle of Avalon.
2. Long before Geoffrey of Monmouth's time Arthur's 'return' was sung of by British bards: according to William of Malmesbury, 'ancient songs fable that he is still to come.'
3. It will be remembered that the daughter of the Evening Star — who danced round the charmed tree as it bent under its load of golden fruit guarded by the dragon — fetched the helm of Hades, or 'the hat of darkness' for Perseus, that he might by its aid cut off the head of the Gorgan in order to turn Atlas to stone by its gaze, for Atlas was tired of holding the heavens and the earth apart.

CHAPTER 2: Pisces
1. This is typical not only of the mystery enshrouding the legend, but also of Arthur Waite's writing. He travelled up to London to see me soon after my Guide was published, and with great sorrow remarked, 'I have spent all my life in quest of the Holy Grail and have not found it; stars and maps did not interest me and now I am too old to revise my life's work.'
2. St John, xix 38.
3. Eusebius Bishop of Caesarea, A.D. 260-340.
4. 'King Solomon's ship' is still to be seen outlined upon King Sedgemoor just below the Twin. It plays an important part in the legends and is the 'boat of the sun' and Argo Navis in the heavens.
5. It is remarkable that during excavations of the Saxon foundations of the Glastonbury Abbey, quite close to 'the old church', twelve skulls were found buried in a stone coffin. I saw them re-placed in it with their bones, re-interred on the same spot.

CHAPTER 3: Aries
1. See 'Argonauts' in *Encyclopedia Britannica*.
2. Moses is often portrayed with ram's horns on his head for this reason.
3. The day that the Lord Mayor of London is elected to office, the city sword is laid in a bed of roses to show that the proceedings are 'sub rosa' at the Aldermans' Court.
4. This was engraved both in Coptic and in Greek on the emerald tablet said to have been found in a cave near Memphis in the hands of the mummy of a priest who was an incarnation of Hermes Trismegistus, the Egyptian Horus — God of boundaries and guide of the dead to the Underworld.
5. Sayce, *Assyria*, p.76.

CHAPTER 4: Taurus
1. Edward Davis, *The Mythology and Rites of the British Druids*, p.508.
2. Excavation at Giza in the neighbourhood of the Mortuary Temple of King Khephren (near the second pyramid) revealed a 'sun-boat' containing the bones of a bull.

CHAPTER 5: Gemini
1. Sir E. A. Wallis Budge, *Amulets and Superstitions*.
2. Recorded by Mary Wheelwright, Santa Fe, New Mexico.
3. See J. S. M. Ward, *Freemasonry and the Ancient Gods* for the illustration of 'The Raising of the Master' and the note on the three 'rods'; see also his chapter on the ancient charges, which hold many of the same traditions as the Arthurian legends.

Ward quotes, 'it began with the first men of the East, who brought it to the West', and adds 'I contend that the brotherhood were descended from a remote period'.

4. I venture to suggest that the hawk, or 'Griffon', standing on the rudder of the ship was laid out in the year 2776 B.C., because in the civil calendar at that very date the July new year was exactly recorded by the heliacal rising of Sirius, which famous star, if traced from the planisphere, falls under the edge of the 'Griffon's' wing, marked by an abundant spring of water. The spring is clearly shown on Grove Lane in the illustration of the 'Griffon' in my *Guide to Glastonbury's Temple of the Stars*.

5. This calf dates him as between 2000 and 4000 B.C. when the Sun was in Taurus.

6. See Sir James Jeans, *The Stars in their Courses*, illustrated by four inspiring photographs of the constellation Orion and its nebulosity.

7. Wolfram von Eschenbach's *Parzival*, translated by Jessie L. Weston, p.262.

8. 'He hath on his thigh a name written, KING OF KINGS, and LORD OF LORDS.' Rev. xix 16.

9. The 5th gate in the 'Tuat', or the kingdom of Osiris (we are told by Wallis Budge, *The Book of the Dead*, p.135-142), held spirit souls with 'thighs seven cubits long.'

10. For this boat see the constellation Argo amongst the stars of the Southern Hemisphere between Orion and Leo; Homer speaks of it as well known to all men; it is Solomon's Ship in Arthurian literature, and in Egypt 'the Boat of Millions of Years' which Ra vacated when he gave his own name to Isis.

11. It should be remembered that the Phoenix was revivified by this 'lapsit exillis', according to the Parzival version, as well as the knights at Monsalvasch.

CHAPTER 7: Virgo

1. 'Hertzeleide' — the mother of the hero of the Grail Quest — dreamed she was 'borne away towards the clouds, and sparks sprang from her floating tresses "mid the fire of the circling sphere" thus she nursed a dragon "that at her breast hung".' The reference to her breast is very marked, for again it says, 'her breasts she tended with the wisdom of mother lore' and 'the queen of Heaven high gave her breast to the dear Lord Jesu.' *Parzival*, p.58.

2. She stands on Wheat Hill near Bab Cary.

CHAPTER 8: Libra

1. Dr S. A. Ionides, *Stars and Men*.

2. J. F. Alberts remarks in regard to this zodiacal circle: 'It has been said that the Church of England is the oldest religion in the world. This may be one of those strange occult sayings that somehow preserves itself in spite of its apparent contradictions. That there is A church in England that is the oldest in the world could be possible, for "church" comes from the same root as does "circle" — *circe*, which we find in several languages.

CHAPTER 9: Sagittarius and Capricornus

1. The Percy manuscript says that King Arthur, whilst boasting to Gawain of his round table, is told by Guenever that she knows of one immeasurably finer, and the palace it stands in is worth all Little Britain besides, but not one word will she say as to where this Table and this goodly building may be: Arthur makes a vow never to sleep two nights in one place till he sees that round table. He sets out on the quest and finds himself in Cornwall.